P

Jeeti

THE SILENT STONING

"Jeeti Pooni's story is an incredible, harrowing true account of courage, resilience, and overcoming. The most triumphant thing Jeeti could ever do is survive her adolescence, and then thoughtfully write this book to share with the world. *The Silent Stoning* is beautifully written, and walks you through an intimate personal account of a childhood enshrouded in betrayal and longing, a tender tale that's a combination of joy and pain, love and shame, and the undoing of a family. The pain is palpable and the victory is in every wave of emotion, as her story unfolds. Jeeti is my hero, a living example of a warrior woman—braver than anyone you'll ever meet.

The Silent Stoning has an intensity that made me feel like I was bearing witness, and in every room with Jeeti. My heart breaks and soars with her, rolls down every hill with her, and climbs back up again, and again, and again—like a big boulder righting a wrong and still gathering speed with life."

Bif Naked platinum record artist and best-selling author of *I, Bificus*

"*The Silent Stoning* is heart-wrenchingly poignant. The innocent and brave sharing of Young Jeeti's journey to comprehend the incomprehensible is as inspiring and beautiful as it is heartbreaking. She eloquently and courageously captures the complex intricacies experienced by sexual abuse victims, and the ripple effect this can have on every aspect of one's self. An illuminating and important read for all striving to truly understand the depth of impacts child sexual abuse has—from clinicians and educators, to parents, partners and friends."

Dr. Joti Samra CEO and founder, MyWorkplaceHealth

Praise for Jeeti Pooni and THE SILENT STONING

"Powerful. Raw. Alarming.

Jeeti takes you on a rollercoaster journey through her heart and mind, a journey so moving that it will shake you out of your comfort zone to fight for your rights and the global injustices of all of our girls."

Mamta Saha founder of Mamta Saha Ltd.,
psychologist and international coach

"A powerful read highlighting the resilience of a victim of child sexual exploitation. Raised in an oppressive and misogynist culture that silenced and shamed victims, Jeeti empowers herself to face her abuse and, in doing so, sets a path of empowerment for survivors of sexual abuse in her community. A story of intense pain and suffering that transforms into a journey of healing."

Parm Johal Criminal Law lawyer and advocate
for victims of child sexual abuse

"*The Silent Stoning* is raw, unfiltered and powerful. Each letter to 'Little Jeeti' or those around her divulge the true story of a young girl who faced years of physical, emotional and sexual abuse. Jeeti Pooni is fearless in her recount of her experiences and fearless in calling out those aspects of a South Asian upbringing that make young girls susceptible to predators. This book will make you angry. This book will make you want to help create change. This book will encourage other women to share their stories. Nothing but praise for Jeeti Pooni and her bravery in putting this book out into the world."

Tina Singh founder of Bold Helmets, occupational
therapist and digital content creator

THE SILENT STONING

THE SILENT STONING

Rediscovering innocence after
childhood sexual abuse

JEETI POONI

TO DESIRE PRESS

Published by To Desire Press

This book is the author's true story as she knows it. It is a memoir.

The author recognizes that others may recall events described in this book differently than she does. The author would like to thank her entire family, extended family and other people portrayed in this book for blessing her with experiences that shaped her to become the person she is today. This book is not intended to hurt any immediate or extended family members or any other people. The author's intent, in publishing this memoir, is to bring to light the passed down cultural norms and beliefs that continue to hinder and suppress women.

This book does not contain medical, psychological, or health advice. It provides information for general and educational purposes only.

Library and Archives Canada Cataloguing in Publication information is available upon request.

ISBN 978-1-7779757-0-8 Paperback
ISBN 978-1-7779757-1-5 Hardcover
ISBN 978-1-7779757-2-2 Ebook

Cover design: Grateful to Bob
Cover author photos: Chelsea Brooke Roisum of CBR Photography
Interior author photo: Grant McAvoy of Image Werx Photography
Interior design: Sandy Kreps of Wildcat Design Studio

Contents

Prologue 1

PART ONE **Innocent**

LETTER 1: I Will Take Care of You 5

LETTER 2: You Will Not Understand At First 13

LETTER 3: You Can Never Be Broken 19

LETTER 4: You Were Born to Shine 27

PART TWO **Confused**

LETTER 5: You Will Be Betrayed 35

LETTER 6: It's Okay to Be Confused 47

LETTER 7: You Are Still Beautiful 61

LETTER 8: You Will Be Taken Advantage Of 67

LETTER 9: You Were Immaculately Groomed 75

PART THREE **Courageous**

LETTER 10: You Are Not Alone 85

LETTER 11: Believe In Miracles 95

LETTER 12: Love Will Find You 99

LETTER 13: You Will Be Silenced 109

LETTER 14: Stand Up For the Truth 115

LETTER 15: You Are a Leader 127

CONTENTS

PART FOUR **Awaken**

LETTER 16: Precious Innocent Princess 139
LETTER 17: Trust the Synchronicities 147
LETTER 18: Expose the Intruder in the Shadows 153
LETTER 19: You Were Right All Along 165
LETTER 20: I Did It, Dad 171
LETTER 21: Strength Is a Muscle 185
LETTER 22: Wake Up, Brother 195
LETTER 23: Woman a Woman's Enemy... Why? 201

PART FIVE **Healing**

LETTER 24: Find Your Spiritual Path 209
LETTER 25: Healing Is a Lifelong Journey 217
LETTER 26: You Can Choose 225
LETTER 27: You Can Trust Women 229
LETTER 28: Awaken to The Great Ancestors 233

Notes to the Reader

LETTER 29: Be the Ripple 241
LETTER 30: You Will Continue 245

Acknowledgments 249

About the Author 251

To Little Jeeti and her innocence,

To Little Kira and Little Salakshana, my sisters,

To my daughters, Maheema and Shia,

And finally, to my niece Chandani and all the children, women, and people who have endured abuse.

Prologue

Dear Reader,

In 2011, the title of the book I had yet to write popped into my mind—*The Silent Stoning*.

It encompassed what I had experienced and witnessed in my life—*the silent stoning* of girls and women. The title was perfect!

As I sat down to write this book six years later, from deep within came the voice encouraging me to write my story in a unique heartfelt way: through a series of letters to Little Jeeti, the young girl I once was and to whom I still have a deep connection. As I wrote the beginning letters in this book to Little Jeeti, I was compelled to also write to my loved ones and others who have impacted my life.

The story of my life unfolds page by page, letter by letter, with details of the most impactful moments of my life and the lessons learned as a result of living through childhood sexual abuse, trauma, immense suffering, and the cultural parameters and belief systems that shaped my life, my mind, and my choices. I appreciate my family, extended family and people portrayed in this book for blessing me with experiences that shaped me to become the person I am today. This book is not intended to hurt any immediate or extended family members or any other person. My intent, in publishing this memoir, is to bring to light the cultural norms and beliefs that continue to hinder and suppress women.

I am so grateful my book has made it into your hands. I am honoured to share the chapters of my life with you. There are many details shared in this book that may be triggering for some of you, especially if you have experienced sexual abuse. I encourage you to find support through a friend, support group, counsellor, therapist, help line, or other networks available in your community as needed. I also recommend that you read this book with a friend, group, or book club for added support, thought-provoking discussions, and healing. If your trauma is more recent or something you have yet to acknowledge or work through, you may want to pause reading through this book until you've sought professional help or emotional support.

As you read through the pages of my lived experiences, know that I am with you wherever you are on your journey.

With Love,

Jeeti

PART ONE

Innocent

LETTER 1

I Will Take Care of You

Dear Little Jeeti,

You were only four years old when you climbed the never ending stairs to board a plane from Delhi airport. You were so scared as you climbed each step on that bright sunny day in April 1973. You were holding your older sister Salakshana's hand while Mom carried your younger sister, Kira, on her hip. It was so hot, nearly 36 degrees Celsius. The sun beamed off the long shiny metal stairs. The noise of the bus that drove you from the terminal and the loud engines of the planes taking off and landing frightened you. You had never seen a plane or an airport before. The environment was so foreign to you, a village girl.

You grew up in Mothada Kalan, a village in Punjab, India, where you rarely saw a car, bus, or motorcycle. You got around mainly by walking, on a bicycle, or in a cart pulled by ox. Here, the ground beneath your feet felt different; it was paved. Even the floors of the airport were different. In your village, you had only seen floors laced with cow dung, straw, and clay. Like the other homes in your village, your house didn't have any electricity or toilets, and water was fetched from a well or a hand water pump. Mom cooked food on a clay structure called a chula (*stove made from clay and bricks*), fueled by cow dung patties and dried corn stalks. To call it a stove would be an overstatement.

That day, your hair was tied back in one braid just like your two sisters. You were all wearing recently stitched clothes your grandfather, Amar Singh Pooni, had custom made for you by a tailor in Goraya, a small city close to your village. You were also wearing shoes, something you were not accustomed to because, in your village, you seldom wore shoes. You walked barefoot inside the house and out in the village streets.

Your stomach was in knots. On the steps of the plane, you were terrified. Perhaps leaving your home in India, not being able to understand where you were going, and knowing you were leaving your teary eyed grandfather behind had something to do with your elevated fear. The truth is, you were a child who was always afraid. You knew not where this fear came from or exactly who drilled it into you. It was just always there.

You stopped and looked back at Mom. Looking at her reassured you everything would be okay; she would always take care of you. Mom did not look tired of carrying Kira and her red plastic hand basket with the square holes up the daunting stairs. She was excited. She was going to reunite with her love, your father, after three years of being separated by a faraway land called Canada.

Mom and Dad had been arranged in marriage at the age of 16. They had no idea what the other one looked like until after they were married. They were both 23 when Dad left for Canada. Now, three years later on the steps of the plane, Mom's excitement was immeasurable and understandably so. At 26 years old, she was going to leave behind a life full of hardship, anguish, and pain. Ever since she got married, she had to work hard to complete her daily chores, waking up before sunrise and going to sleep well after sunset. She was beautiful, smart, responsible, and a strong workhorse, exactly what Grandfather wanted in a daughter-in-law for his household.

Grandfather was tall, slender, and belonged to the Kuka

(*pronounced Koo-ka*) Namdhari Sikh Punjabi faith, so he always wore traditional white cotton clothes: a turban, kurta (*long, loose shirt*), and pajami (*tight-fitting, skinny pants*). He was the head of the household and took care of the daily needs. You loved your grandfather. You believed you were his favourite grandchild. The two of you shared a bond that even you didn't comprehend at the time. You just knew that, around him, you felt safe, loved, and protected. When he used to come home for lunch after working on the family farm and running errands, he would share his lunch with you. He used to play with you and your sister, Kira. Your youngest Phua (*meaning Dad's sister*) told you he never used to share his lunch with any of the other grandkids. So yes, you definitely were his favourite.

Your family was not very well off in India. By the age of 22, Dad had fathered four children: your older sister Salakshana, Umba (your brother who died at only nine days old), you, and Kira, who was just an embryo in Mom's stomach when Dad left India. Daughters are a burden in Indian culture, and the pressure of having to give dowry is immense. Grandfather was a visionary who took risks. In 1970, when you were only a year and a half old, he sent Dad, his workhorse, out to Canada in hopes of economic prosperity for all the Pooni family. Dad was expected not only to share his wealth but also to help his relatives immigrate to Canada. From a very young age, Dad worked hard on his family farm in India, so Grandfather knew Dad was the most responsible of all of his sons.

Once in Canada, Dad was to get a job and send money back to India to help feed the entire Pooni family, which consisted of Mom, Salakshana, Kira, you, Grandfather, Grandmother, Thaya (*meaning Dad's older brother*) and his family, and Chacha (*meaning Dad's younger brother*). Thanks to the policies of Canadian Prime Minister, Pierre Elliot Trudeau, Dad was granted permanent residency in Canada. Dad did as he was obliged and made his father proud. He found a labor intensive job at Lignum Limited, a lumber mill in Williams Lake, British Columbia working on the chainsaw.

Once Dad was settled and became a permanent Canadian resident, Grandfather decided to send Chacha out to Canada, too. Chacha arrived in 1972. Of course, Grandpa hoped Chacha would follow in Dad's footsteps, getting a job to send money back home. Grandfather had no desire to send Mom, you, and your sisters to Canada. He saw you all as a burden on Dad. If you were in Canada, Dad would have to provide you with food, shelter, and clothing, an added expense that meant he would not be able to send as much money back home to the village. Grandfather wanted to buy land to expand his small family farm. But Dad was sponsoring Chacha's permanent residency application, which was based on a point system. The application would hold more points and would fast track Chacha's permanent residence status if Dad was a family man in Canada. So, he told Grandfather it was vital to send Mom, Salakshana, Kira, and you over to Canada.

That's how you finally ended up on the plane to Canada.

You had four seats in a row in the middle section of the plane: one each for Mom, Salakshana, you and Kira. Kira mostly sat in Mom's lap. Everything about being on a plane was foreign to you—the inside of the tubular plane itself, the air hostesses, the seats, the seat belts. You had never seen a seatbelt before and found it difficult to fasten.

You had a night's stay in Tokyo. Mom didn't understand the language and couldn't communicate in anything other than Punjabi. A woman travelling on our flight helped Mom use food vouchers to order food at the hotel. Hunger pains jabbed at your stomach as you waited for that meal in your hotel room. Lying on the bed, you cried off and on, repeatedly asking Mom when the food was coming. You bounced up full of delight when you heard the knock on the door. You stared at the Japanese person who brought in your meal, as you had never seen a Japanese person before. You were so excited to eat, but your excitement was short-lived. It was some kind of rice mixed with what Mom said were worms (though looking back, it must have been shrimp or something). You were all vegetarian, and you girls had never eaten meat of any kind. So, Mom told you not to eat the worms, only the rice. Sadly, the rice tasted awful; it was nothing like what you ate in your village. You had a few bites and fell asleep hungry.

Dad picked you all up at the Vancouver airport on April 24, 1973. Salakshana, Kira, and you were too shy and scared to greet or give hugs to Dad, a person you didn't remember. You hid behind Mom. You drove straight to Williams Lake, a 7 1/2-hour journey by car back then. You all were so tired. Salakshana and you sat in the back seat of Dad's humongous yellow car, a four-door Dodge. You were afraid of him and spoke only to Mom to ask when you would be home.

Prior to your arrival into Canada, Dad had bought a three-bedroom brown bungalow house on the corner of the street. It was across from Marie Sharpe Elementary School and the ice arena and within walking distance from downtown. The best part was that you lived only a two minute walk from Kiwanis Park, which had an outdoor wading pool, swings, teeter-totter, slide, and monkey bars. Overwaitea Foods and the Alston movie theatre were close by, too. It was a great place for a family.

You were one of the few Indian families who lived in town, as it was more expensive than living on the outskirts. Most Indian families lived in Glendale, an area that had not been incorporated into the town yet. You lived with your older Phua (Dad's sister), her husband, their three children, Chacha, and two other young adult males who had recently immigrated to Canada. Phua and her family shared one room, and Mom, Dad, your sisters, and you shared the second room. Chacha and the two males, Bikkar and Rai, shared the other room. There was only one washroom for all 13 of you.

You and your sisters adapted quickly to your new lifestyle in this predominantly white town. There were so many things in your house you had never seen before, including a chesterfield, a black and white TV, a telephone, a fridge, a stove, a record player, and much more. You learned how to use the sink, the toilet, taps, and toilet paper. You also started to brush your teeth and got your first haircuts. You even got to eat ice cream and popsicles for the first time! You saw your first Bollywood movie, and you immediately fell in love with the beautiful actresses and actors, the songs, the dancing, the bold jewelry, and the colourful fabrics of the saris and ghagra cholis (*traditional Indian women's clothing*). The screen was huge with burgundy velvet curtaining, and the adorned actresses lit up the entire theatre and your heart. You thought the actors all lived behind the burgundy curtaining and could see you watching from the other side of the screen. You thought that if the villains saw you sticking out your tongue at them, they would stop being mean to the heroine and leave her alone.

You were like a kid in a candy store then. Canada was so exciting. You watched English TV shows even though you didn't understand the language. *Brady Bunch, Good Times, Sanford and Son, Hawaii Five-O, Mannix, Star Trek, Six Million Dollar Man, Kojak, Columbo, The Streets of San Francisco, Flintstones, Bugs Bunny,* and old western movies were among your favourites. Of course, you saw all the heroes on TV and film in Dad. Sometimes he reminded you of a brown version of Captain Kirk from *Star Trek*. Other times, he reminded you of Dharmendra, a Bollywood actor you had seen in Indian films. Dad would pose in front of the bathroom mirror, which had openable mirrored doors, and have pictures taken of himself. He would adjust the mirrored doors so the camera would capture his many reflections. I stood outside of the washroom door admiring Dad and watching him pose. He always looked so handsome. He took pictures of Mom and you girls, too. You were excited when he took pictures of you and your sisters dancing to *Heer Ranja* songs in your living room. You girls twirled with Mom's georgette chunni (*scarf*) or shawl on your heads pretending you were actresses just like in the Bollywood movies. You felt so much joy and excitement. You learned how to stretch your imagination and tap into endless creativity. You also learned how females seemed to have to be beautiful, perfect, obedient, and submissive. In the movies, they would be punished and cast out if they weren't.

Of course, it wasn't all magic and excitement in those early days in Canada. At times you felt a little confused. You had to get used to living with Dad and other members in the house. You and your sisters did not know English; you only spoke Punjabi. Chacha did not want you to call him "Chacha," the word in Punjabi for a younger uncle on Dad's side of the family. He wanted you to call him "Uncle," which was very odd for you and your sisters. Back in your village, he had always been your Chacha. There, you girls would have been punished for being impolite if you had called him something else. Of course, you were very obedient and always complied with the adults in your family. So, in Canada, you always tried to do as you were asked.

Salakshana was obedient, too. Kira, on the other hand, was a very curious and rambunctious child. Dad registered both of his obedient daughters in summer school to learn English. (Kira was too young anyhow.) He knew the importance of you girls learning English quickly in your new country. Summer school was full of newly arrived children from India. Even your instructors were Indian. You played games you had never played before to help you get acquainted with each other and the language. You also got to go for a picnic and camping at the lake. It was fun, and you and your sisters quickly learned English, only to be reprimanded later by Dad. He still wanted you to speak Punjabi, not English, at home.

In September, Dad took you to the school across the street from your house to meet the principal. Dad and the principal chatted in English. The principal tried talking to you, asking your name. You were extremely shy and too scared to respond. You hid behind Dad, looking for safety behind his legs. Because of this, the principal did not register you into the school. You would have to go to Chilcotin Road Elementary, a school 6.8 km out of town.

Salakshana was sent to a school in Glendale, 4 km away, where all the new Indian immigrant kids were enrolled.

You didn't know why you and your sister had to be separated in two different schools. Dad reprimanded you for not answering the principal at that first meeting. You felt a huge lump in your throat as the overwhelming feeling of having disappointed him took you over.

"She didn't take you because she thinks you don't know English. You should have answered her," he said. "You can speak."

With Love,

Jeeti

LETTER 2

You Will Not Understand At First

Dear Little Jeeti,

It was the first week in February 1974, a year after you came to Canada, that you and your family moved to your new red and white house up the hill on 4th Avenue North in Williams Lake.

You, Mom, Salakshana, and Kira could not contain your excitement. This house was much more beautiful, bigger, and newer than your old house. It had huge front and back yards for you and your sisters to play tag, chase butterflies, do cartwheels, roll in somersaults, and find four leaf clovers until sunset. There was a fire hydrant in the front you could jump off of, a large sundeck you could twirl, dance, catch, and eat snowflakes on, and a driveway large enough for you girls to ride your bikes and play with your skipping ropes—singles, doubles, angels and devils, or Chinese skipping. Mom could have her large vegetable garden in the back yard and even a swing set for you girls. The numerous trees would definitely provide shade in the hot summer sun.

Inside, the house had two real wood-burning fireplaces accented with stones and a raised black slate hearth. You couldn't believe you could have a real fire. The yellow kitchen with its olive green fridge and stove, countless brown cabinets all around the top and bottom of the four walls, large cream laminate countertops with a yellowy gold marble pattern, and an island large enough to seat all five of you at its breakfast bar seating was so inviting. The living room and dining room were spacious, too. The house was carpeted with a green shag rug that could transform into green grass under your feet while you danced like a Bollywood actress or become your friend in moments of boredom as you twirled its never ending strands between your tiny fingers. The washroom was huge with a large countertop the three of you sisters could sit on. The expansive mirrored cabinets on the wall were perfect for you to sit in front of while you applied Mom's makeup, put on her Indian jewelry, and imagined yourself as a Bollywood actress just like in the movie posters. The pink bathtub, sink, and toilet all sat looking happy and pretty. The walls surrounding the bathtub were covered in countless one inch tiles. You could run your fingers along the grout as if you were following a maze while bathing. The house even had a second washroom with an olive green sink and toilet in the master bedroom. It had three bedrooms upstairs and a large spacious basement. One bedroom for your parents, one for Uncle, and one for you and your sisters. The house was perfect and full of colour, just like your box of Crayola crayons.

You, Salakshana, Kira, and Mom all loved that home. It felt as if the joyous feeling you found there would last forever. It felt like the beginning of something, but you didn't know what.

One day, when you, Salakshana, and Kira were playing in the big backyard of your new house, a young, fat Italian neighbourhood boy started throwing rocks at the three of you. He stood in the yard next to you, repeatedly throwing stones and calling you all names. You and Salakshana ducked, but Kira stood straight. She was too young to know better. One of the rocks hit her forehead and cracked it open. She screamed and cried at the top of her lungs as she bled. The boy took off. All you and your sisters wanted to do was play. You wanted to become friends with other kids in your new neighbourhood. Why someone would throw rocks at you and call you names is something you didn't understand, but you knew then that you didn't want to be that boy's friend.

Another time you and Salakshana were walking home from school, the same boy would not stop making fun of you two. Salakshana got so mad she finally hit him straight in the face with her school textbook. He never bothered you girls again.

There were others that took his place though. There was the white girl who pulled your pigtail when you were six years old one morning as you were walking to school. There was the white boy and his friends who blocked your path with his bike and said, "Go home, Hindu." There was the boy who repeatedly blocked the door to the school entrance so you couldn't get in. In short, it wasn't always easy.

You felt hurt, terrified, unsafe, different, unwanted, and out of place. It made you feel as if you didn't belong. You didn't understand why these kids wanted you to go "home" or the meaning of the word Hindu. It turns out that the list of things you wouldn't understand would only grow in that time of your life.

You were around six when Dad rented the basement suite to an Indian family. Dad called the man Pago. He was about Dad's age, around 28. He was skinny, unattractive, dark skinned, clean shaven, and smelled like cigarettes. He moved in with his wife and daughter, who was your age. The door inside the house leading into the basement suite was never locked. Mom and Dad had a trusting relationship with the tenants. You and your sisters were even allowed to go down and play with the little girl if you wanted to.

When your parents were gone to buy groceries, Pago would come upstairs and sit on the sofa while you would be watching TV. Sometimes Salakshana would be sitting on the other end of the sofa, and he would lie down with his legs facing her, tucking his feet under her thighs. She would wiggle and move as far to the corner of the sofa as she could, looking very uncomfortable and scared. When it happened, she would frown, and her eyes would bulge out. Other times he would go into the kitchen and touch her budding breasts as she made roti for you and Kira. You didn't know why she always had a scared look on her face every time he came upstairs, but you were both uneasy having Pago upstairs without your parents. Salakshana told Mom what Pago was doing to her, but Mom didn't do anything about it. All she did was tell Salakshana not to go to him.

One day, Pago had you in his bedroom downstairs. He must have asked you to come into his room, and of course, you were obedient. That's what children were supposed to do. The room was very basic with one window and not very much furniture. His bed was in the center of the bedroom. You know because Pago put you on the bed.

Everything was quiet in the house. You couldn't hear anyone. That's what you were thinking when he took off your pants and underwear. Then he took off his clothes. He was skinny and dark, and you felt very uncomfortable. He spread your legs. Scared, you lay in complete silence, frozen. He spit into his hand and put the saliva on his penis. He also put saliva from his wet hand onto your genital area. He leaned his body on top of you and glided his penis back and forth against your genitals.

"Swad ondha?" he asked you, meaning, "Do you feel pleasure?"

You shook your head. The gliding back and forth of his penis on top of your genitals was hurting your entire private area. The pressure of something hard against your genitals was very uncomfortable. He glided back and forth a few more times and then, he just stopped. He put your clothes back on and said, "Don't tell anyone. Don't tell my wife. She will say we are stupid."

You did as you were told. You never told anyone, not even your sisters or Mom. You didn't really know what happened or what Pago had done to you at the time. So, you carried on with life as a 6-year-old girl—cheerful, playful, loving, and obedient.

To cope, you shut out the incident from your mind and let yourself be swept up by the Bollywood world.

Your imagination soared without bounds. One day you were a Bollywood actress. The next day you were Cleopatra or Scarlett O'Hara. It was the Bollywood melodies you danced to daily pretending to be Asha Parekh, Hema Malini or Mumtaz. You loved escaping into your imaginary Bollywood world, dancing to your favourite 1970's Hindi movie songs from *Aan Milo Sajana, Dharmatma, Aya Sawan Jhoom Ke, Neel Kamal,* Pakastani version of *Heer Ranja*, and so many more. You would pull up and twist your t-shirt to mimic a sari blouse and wrap yourself in a khesi (*traditional Punjabi blanket*) to pretend it was an elaborate silk sari in the brightest colours—yellow, magenta, lime green, orange, or whatever hue came to your mind. Your little girl heart beat quickly as you sang, twirled around and around, swivelled your hips, and moved your arms with grace as the record player dropped one record after another. Your feet would take you rapidly from one end of the living room to the other, on to the sofa, back down to the green shag carpet, and then on to the cold black slate fireplace hearth. You pretended you were on a mountain top or in a luscious field just like in the movies adorned in elaborate Indian jewelry. You imagined dancing around the smiling, handsome, and loving male actors, just as the actresses did.

You performed and performed to your heart's delight. You didn't pick up on the wiring of subliminal cultural messages and the dark shades of indoctrination embedded in each song and film. You were oblivious to it all, just like you were unaware of what Pago had unleashed on you.

In your Bollywood, you were safe.

With Love,

Jeeti

LETTER 3

You Can Never Be Broken

Dear Kira,

Salakshana and I were submissive and deathly afraid of the adults in our house. You? Not so much. You were true to your innocence, curiosity, and vibrant self. You had no qualms in standing up for yourself.

As children we were always punished if we did something wrong. One of the first punishments I remember was in our old brown house soon after we came from India. I don't remember what we were being punished for, but I remember the punishment. We were forced to climb down into the dark, dingy dugout basement as the wooden trap door and its latch were closed on top of our heads. The trap door was on the floor and used to get down into the unfinished basement that had narrow, steep wooden stairs. It was so dark and spooky. I cried as I crouched on the third step of the stairs holding on for dear life while you crouched on the step above. I could see nothing.

"Don't cry," you told me.

You were a brave three-year-old girl comforting your older sister. What you didn't know was that I was slapped and locked in a dark room as a girl your age in India. It was my punishment for eating dirt, so now as a five-year-old I was deathly terrified of being abandoned and locked up in dark, spooky places. I saw you forced into this dingy basement a few times. Dumbbells were placed on the trap door as weight so you couldn't push open the door from underneath. I heard you cry at the top of your lungs, pounding on the trap door. I heard the latch rattle and the dumbbells shake, dancing to an eerie tune of their own. I watched helplessly. There was nothing I could do to help you, my little baby sister.

Kira, you were about four years old in our new house when I remember you yelling and screaming while you were held by your ankles and dangled upside down off the staircase banister.

"I am going to let you go head first."

That was the threat hurled at you as you flailed your arms and body. I don't remember what you were being punished for, but again, I remember the punishment. I remember all the punishments you and I received together—a slap across the face, a wooden spoon or belt across the hand, a whip from a special stick (a tree branch from our backyard), being tied up and separated in a corner for what seemed like hours and not being allowed to speak to each other.

Of course, these pale in comparison to the punishments you received alone. I know because I was always made to watch whenever a punishment was laid on you.

"Come here," came the command in a rude, unloving Punjabi male voice. "Stand here and don't move."

I would always obey. I would stand still, frozen and silent with a lump in my throat. I was always trying my hardest not to cry in those moments.

I remember watching in horror on another occasion when you were tied up with our pink skipping rope and put into the bathtub as the drain was plugged and the tap turned on full blast.

"I am going to drown you," came the threat.

You were crying and screaming at the same time. Your body squirmed as strong, hairy arms held you down. You fought back with all your might. I stood by the doorway, holding my breath and hoping you would be let go. I silently wished you would be quiet so he would let you go. I felt guilty for having to go fetch the rope for him. I felt so powerless. I wished I could untie the skipping rope—the very rope Salakshana, you, and I had so much fun skipping outside with.

This is not what it was supposed to be used for, I thought to myself. Powerlessly, I watched the water rise inch by inch. I was only seven years old at the time, and my fear was at an all-time high. It was dreadful. I thought you were really going to drown. I thought you were going to die.

Another time we were in the unfinished spooky laundry room downstairs. It was my least favourite part of the house. It held a gloominess, an unpleasantness in the air of many dark memories to come. There, you were put in the dryer with the door forcibly closed on you after the attempt to put you in the washing machine had failed. You fought so hard to stay out, but the force on the other side was too powerful.

"I am going to turn on the dryer," the angry voice yelled as you kicked and screamed from inside. You pushed the door open a little, but it was closed shut on you again and again. You continued to scream on the top of your tiny lungs. All I could do the whole time was hope the moment would be over. To my relief, the dryer was never turned on. I never did like being in the dark and dreary laundry room, but it became forever dark and dreary for me after that day.

There was also a time, Kira, when I believed your head was going to be cut off with a pair of scissors. You were around six years old on the living room floor being held down forcibly. Both your wrists were held by one hand, and there was a pair of strong legs locked around you to prevent you from wiggling and escaping your captor. One arm held you down while the other held a pair of scissors wide open in the opposite hand.

"I am going to cut your throat," said the angry ruthless voice.

I believed the threats. You were loud with your screams. You squirmed and thrashed with all your might as the scissors came closer to your neck. You moved your face side to side. One of the blades of the scissors nicked the left side of your face, close to your eye. You bled. I did my best to hold back my tears, afraid I too would be punished for crying. Of course, I could not hold them back. I cried as quietly as I could. I felt the warm tears rolling down my face. You were let go eventually, but somehow you were still the one who got into even more trouble for getting cut.

"You could have been blinded," said the voice. I didn't know as a child what was worse: being blind from one eye or having your throat cut off. Both outcomes seemed bad.

Another severe punishment came to you when you were six years old. It was 10:00 in the morning, and we were playing by the top of the staircase in our new house. Our Uncle had just woken up. He came out of his bedroom in his red underwear and was headed toward the washroom in the hall. Dad had told him countless times not to come out in his briefs, but Uncle didn't care. As he came down the hall, you said the word "dumb" or "dummy." I don't know if you were just saying the word out loud or if you were calling me a name, but Uncle thought you were talking to him. He said something mean in Punjabi and tried to grab you. You ran through the kitchen, out the back door of the house, and straight through the backyard. You went under the barbed wire fence and into the back alley. Almost six feet tall, he followed, injuring himself when he jumped over the barbed wire fence out back. Halfway down the dirt road alley, you stopped running. I don't know why you did that. I'm guessing deep inside you knew you would be in bigger trouble if you kept running. He caught up to you. He grabbed you, slapped you, and dragged you all the way home. I could hear you crying out loud the whole way.

He dragged you inside and into the living room. Then, he went over to the coffee table, unscrewed one of its round legs, and beat you over and over again with it. Both of our Massis (*Massi meaning*

Mom's sister) who had recently immigrated from India were watching. I watched too, hiding behind one of our Massis. We were both crying. I wanted someone to do something. I wanted him to stop. I could not understand why no one would stop him. Finally, one of our Massis spoke up. Through tears, she asked him to stop. He did not listen; he continued beating you. Once he let you go, this Massi hugged you and cried while she was putting oil on the bulges on your arms and knees. The sadness followed me like a shadow for the rest of the day.

Uncle made it a big joke. He laughed about how he gave you three knees because you didn't listen. I didn't like this part of Uncle. I only liked the nice part of him. A year or two earlier, he took me to my first car wash. I sat frozen as the machine rumbled and sprayed the car with soap and water. Everything shook, along with my insides. I'd never seen anything like it before! I was scared. He then took me to the Mini Mart. I had never been there before either. He said I could buy a chocolate bar. No one in my family had taken me out to buy a chocolate bar, so I didn't even know how to pick one. Our parents hardly bought us chocolate, and if we did get some, the whole family would share one bar with Mom administering all of us a small piece.

"Have the Hershey," Uncle said as he pointed to one of the shelves of the Mini Mart. The wrapper looked exactly like the one I'd seen in a TV commercial.

"Take some for your sisters, too," he continued.

I slowly picked up two more. I felt so special that Uncle had taken me out that day. I knew I was his favourite niece.

I don't know if you remember, Kira, but it was a year later when another one of our Massis immigrated from India and came to live with us. You were seven years old. She used to yell at us in her loud, rude voice. Her Punjabi was ruder than Dad's. Like many of the other adults in our house, she was always quick to yell at you, me, and Salakshana, eager to slap us at any moment. I don't know why Mom and Dad didn't set any boundaries with the grown ups in our home. I don't know why they allowed the adults to discipline us in whichever way they deemed appropriate.

This Massi also had numerous verbal altercations with Mom, Dad, and Uncle. Once during bedtime, she pounced off the bed to slap you as you ran toward the bedroom door. She caught up to you by the door. As she tried to grab you, your face hit the edge of the door. Your eyebrow was cut open, and you were instantly bleeding. You cried out so loud that Mom heard the commotion and came out of her bedroom, saw what was going on and reprimanded our Massi for hurting you. Mom had to take you to the hospital for stitches that night.

Kira, it was horrible having to watch you suffer and endure so much trauma. I don't know what was more traumatic: being punished in the ways that you were or being forced to watch the entirety of each episode from beginning to end like I was. I can't even begin to imagine what you felt inside during these horrific punishments. All I know is the terror, shame, guilt, and powerlessness I felt inside every time we were punished.

Could it be that the punishments administered on us 3 girls were less severe than what the adults had experienced through their childhood? After all, the adults themselves told us our paternal grandmother suffered from some sort of mental illness. They told us stories of how she verbally abused and beat her children with the wet giant ropes used to draw water from the well. When Grandmother's manic episodes got severe, Grandfather would take her to Goraya, the nearest city, to get her electrical brain shock therapy. They said her mom (our Dad's grandmother) was even worse. Whenever she would come visit, she would bring her own "special stick" to beat her grandchildren. It was common practice during our parent's childhood for adults to beat children in order to teach them obedience to authority.

Even then, what was done to us, especially you, was not right. There is nothing you could have done as a little child that warranted the punishments you received. The adults around us could have chosen differently. They could have allowed our innocent curiosity to play out so we could grow into empowered confident girls. Instead they chose harsh punishment to control our behaviour, break us down, and tame us to conform to their will.

Wonderful Kira, what I do know is that these cruel methods were trying to strip you, me, and Salakshana of our power and worth. They were trying to make us obedient and subservient girls; this was and is the norm in our Indian culture. The deep underlying psychology behind it was not only that we would be better daughters, wives, and daughters-in-law if we were broken, but ultimately that we would be subservient to men forever, upholding the thriving of men and their power in our culture.

My darling sister, I still remember your little baby hands stuck out straight forward and flat with palms facing up as we stood side by side in a conforming line. We were all waiting for the wrath of a wooden spoon, belt, or whatever instrument was about to be used for punishment. And I knew that if your tiny five-year-old frame could confidently stand up to the might of Goliath, so could I one day.

I remember your stubbornness when we were ordered to bow our heads and not look into the eyes of the male who held the power. You would stare back with your bright wide eyes, locking your gaze and refusing to listen. You were stubborn, challenging him like a ram. The full weight of the slap on your cheek sent you flying. You were made to stand up again as the angry voice repeated the instructions, all the while knowing deep inside you would not be controlled.

It is that resilient spark within you that kept my own flame lit.

You, Kira, helped me persevere until my time would come to challenge authority.

With Love,

Jeeti

LETTER 4

You Were Born to Shine

Dear Pago, Parmar, Papa, and Priest,

What a coincidence your names all begin with the letter "P."

Just like the word pedophile.

Parmar, I was seven years old when you took me, my two sisters, and your two young little daughters (around ages four and six) out for a ride in your car. You asked me to sit beside you on the long front bench seat of your car. It was dark outside. You wanted us to see the night view of our small town. You parked somewhere, turned off the car, and told your daughter to go to the back seat.

"Stay in the back seat," you ordered all of the girls except me.

In the darkness you forced my head toward your lap and forced my mouth onto something hard, warm, and stinky.

"Suck on it," you whispered in Punjabi.

I pulled my head away from your lap. I did not know what had just happened, but I knew I did not want it to happen again. Lucky for me, the other girls did not obey you, and some of them came into the front seat again, one of them being my sister Kira. You quickly zipped up your pants as you scolded the girls for being disobedient.

You did not stop there. On occasion, your hand would graze my flat chest, and you would squeeze as if you were squeezing breasts. I was nine years old when you asked me to help you put oil on the lawn mower. You took me into your garage and put me on top of the bumper of your car, pulled down my pants, bent me over, and tried to shove your oil-laced penis into my buttocks. I felt a sharp pain, pulled myself away, and started to cry. My lucky stars must have been shining bright that afternoon because I was spared when Salakshana, Kira, and your daughters opened the garage door. You shouted at them to close the door and go away. You pulled up my pants, took me off of the car, gave me candy, and told me not to cry. You started doing something to yourself instead, quickly moving your hand back and forth until it resulted in streaks of white fluid on the cement floor.

"What is that?" I asked you.

"Nothing," you replied, zipping up your pants as you finally let me go.

Papa, I was seven years old when you joined our family in Canada. With you from India came two of my Massis. My sisters and I were filled with joy when you, Papa, our Mom's father, arrived. You came at an exciting time in our lives because Mom had given birth to a son, my baby brother Jesse. Mom and Dad were ecstatic to finally have a son, a boy they had been waiting for who would have a long life. He would be followed a year later by another baby, my sister Rakhee.

You, Papa, reminded me of Santa Claus with your white beard, mustache, and big fat round stomach. You would allow me and Kira to sit on your stomach and bounce up and down. You would throw us over in somersaults. You allowed me to braid your beard and taught us how to play cards. Dad and Uncle never played with us girls, so playing with you, Papa, was fun.

At least it was in the beginning.

Once, Kira and I were playing in our room while you lay on my bed. I started bouncing on your stomach. As I was bouncing and giggling, you asked me to kiss you. I gave you a sweet innocent peck on your cheek.

"Here," you said, pointing to your lips. I leaned forward and gave you a peck on your hairy lips.

"Put your tongue in my mouth," you commanded.

My smile and joy left abruptly as I complied. Your tongue tugged at my tongue. I was so scared. It felt as if my tongue was being pulled right out of my throat. It seemed you had sucked most of my face into your mouth. I felt your gums. It was then I realized not only did you have bad breath, but you had no teeth. I squirmed with all my might until I was able to pull my tongue out of your mouth. It was disgusting.

Sadly, the disgust did not end there. You used your hands to slide me off of your stomach and onto your pelvis.

"Move back and forth," you said as your hands forced my hips back and forth.

I felt something hard and uncomfortable underneath me. It was not fun moving back and forth. I jumped up and down instead.

I don't remember playing on your stomach ever again.

Priest, I don't know much about you. I remember only that you were an unattractive, short, and scrawny turbaned Punjabi Sikh man in a kurta pajama. You were the priest of the Guru Nanak Sikh Temple in Williams Lake, a gurdwara my Dad and the Sikh community members help built from personal donations in 1974 for the good of the community.

It was a bright, sunny day after the Sunday prayer. All the young kids headed to the tiny old little house located in the parking lot of the temple. The house belonged to the temple. In it was a library and a room for you, Priest. The children were all excited to go to the house to play, to learn how to pray, and to look at the books in the library. I had never been before. There were about 15 children there in total, including my little sister Kira and a few of my friends. Inside the house, you gathered us all in the living room

which had a bed on one side and a teaching area on the other side. You never let us go into the library; instead, you had us chant a Sikh prayer (*Mool Mantar*) using words I had not heard before. It was much different than the Lord's Prayer we recited at school every morning. Yours began something like this:
(the meaning I was later told)

"*Ek onkar*	There is one universal God
Sat nam	Truth is his name
Karta purakh..."	He is the creator...

Bored, some of us children started to jump on the bed. You would pick a girl one by one and throw her on the bed. You only picked up the little girls, telling the boys they were too heavy. There was a little girl around two years old in a dress who kept crying in your arms every time you picked her up. When it was my turn, you picked me up and placed me on the crook of your arm. I was wearing a beautiful new red dress my mom had bought me. We hardly ever got new clothes, so this dress was a rare treat. I felt like a princess.

Until you shoved your finger into my panties and up into my vagina. I flinched when I felt pain and discomfort. Immediately after your mission was accomplished, you threw me onto the bed. You proceeded with the next little girl, over and over again. I saw blood on your fingers shortly after. When I asked you what it was, you told me it was nothing. To this day, I do not know if that blood was mine or how many other girls it may have belonged to. I do know once the gurdwara became aware of your behaviour you were sent away to serve at a gurdwara in another community.

Pedophiles. The whole lot of you. Little did I know you all left me scarred. Etched with repugnant memories that will forever remain embedded in my mind and body. Trauma and sensations so deep no child can understand.

Despite the fact you held the power, I continued to live my

life as a vibrant, creative, imaginative, and loving Little Jeeti. Not knowing the ugliness of what you had inflicted upon me, I shined in my brilliance. I did not yet understand what you'd taken from me in my childhood.

Today you are all dead, Papa, Pago, Parmar, and I assume you too, Priest. You all died of cancer.

My, you all share a lot in common.

Truly,

Jeeti

PART TWO

Confused

LETTER 5

You Will Be Betrayed

Dear Dad,

I remember how excited I was when Mom said, "Manjit is coming from India."

Manjit was my cousin, your nephew, your second oldest sister's son. He was 20 years old and always nice to me. Of course, I was thrilled at the idea of his arrival. Finally, my sisters and I would have an older cousin to play with. It would be just like having a big brother!

You made it crystal clear, Dad, that Manjit was a brother and that all of us children had to call him "Paaji." *(It's commonly spelled as Bhaji, meaning "brother" in Punjabi. I like to spell it just like I hear it: Paaji.)* You made sure to emphasize the suffix "-ji" to convey the utmost respect a brother deserved in our culture. Your furrowed brows when you spoke left no doubt of physical punishment if we ever disrespected him by calling him by his first name. It came without any question that whatever Paaji said, we girls had to obey. You further drilled in the fact Manjit was a brother by having all your daughters tie a Rakhri *(a bracelet made of various threads)* on his wrist for Rakhri Day the week he arrived. It was a cultural ceremony to emphasize the sacred bond of love and protection by a brother. While tying the silk thread on our brother's wrist, us sisters were supposed to pray for his well being, and he was supposed to promise to take care of us as his sisters.

Paaji mixed into our family very quickly like a loving big brother. He received so much love from the adults, and he liked to play with us children a lot. He was fun, so we all loved playing with him. We were still young when he arrived: I was 11, Salakshana was 16, Kira was 10, Jesse was 4, and your youngest daughter, Rakhee, was under 3.

All the adults and children in the Pooni household opened their loving hearts to Paaji and gave him deep respect. Everyone ensured to include Paaji in conversations, family games, Bollywood movie nights, and any family holidays or functions. Paaji was shy, quiet, and obedient. He didn't cause any trouble. He would sit on the sofa with his head bowed, never talking much. He didn't drink or go out. He was always home, except when he went to work or to English classes.

He was well taken care of in your loving home, Dad. You treated him like your own son. You even treated him better than your own daughters. He never had to mow the lawn, help in the garden, sweep the driveway, shovel the snow, take out the garbage, or wash the cars. He didn't have to do any household chores like we, your daughters, did. You and Uncle showered him with more love and kindness than any of us received. Every day he feasted on eggs, roasted chicken legs and thighs, pork chops, hamburgers, or T-bone steaks while your daughters had to eat roti with dhal *(lentils cooked Indian style)* or sabji *(cooked Indian vegetable dish)*. Your entire fridge was stocked for him with creamed milk, yogurt, eggs, and fine meats. You went over and beyond to support him, Dad, including his desire to become a wrestler. You hoped he would make a good champion, going to national and international tournaments or even the Olympics. You later had him train with Kartar Singh, a renowned Indian wrestler from Punjab.

You used to come home from work and ask Paaji about his

day, something you never asked any of your daughters. You used to smile and laugh with him as you talked. You took him for his first haircut, enrolled him in English classes, taught him how to drive, and more. You never yelled or punished him, not even once. It was as if he was a golden child to you. He won your heart and your trust without even doing anything to earn it. Perhaps it was so culturally ingrained in you to privilege only males in the family. Only they deserved your blind respect. Perhaps in your subconscious mind, he reminded you of Umba, the son you didn't get to see or hold.

It was mid-October, two months after Paaji came into our home, when you and Mom left for a three-month trip to India with Salakshana, Kira, and Jesse. You left Rakhee and me behind because I had gone the year before and you thought Rakhee was too young to travel. Before you left, you had a conversation with me in the kitchen. You were sitting on the stool and I was standing in front of you while Paaji was standing to your side.

"You have to obey your aunts and uncles," you told me. "You have to be a good girl. Obey your Paaji. Come straight home after school. No playing with boys."

I was still a little girl, so it felt awkward and embarrassing hearing you say these things. You hadn't lectured me in this way before. I felt a certain sadness when you said that. I loved to play on the school playground with my friends after school. It meant so much to me to play on the big toys, go down the big slide, sit on the round tire swing, and slide down the fireman's pole as everyone chased each other and played tag.

"Aday utay akh rukhi," you told Paaji, meaning, *"Keep an eye on her, take care of her."*

I nodded, reassuring you I would be a "good girl". You left me in the hands of adults you loved and trusted, my Massi married to Uncle and two other Massis and their husbands (my Massers) who not only lived in our house but also loved your family.

I felt sad waving goodbye to you, Mom, and my siblings as you boarded the Greyhound bus to Vancouver. My heart was sinking into my stomach. I was being left behind. I wanted to go too and didn't understand why you didn't take me with you. Paaji held my hand as I waved to all of you.

"Don't cry," he said as we walked back to our car.

I sat in the back seat with a lump in my throat, pushing back tears. I didn't say a word on the ride home. The Massi driving the car said a few words to console me, but I didn't know how I was going to live every day without them. Three months seemed like an eternity. There was a strange quietness inside of me without my family nearby. When we got home, the house felt strangely dark, quiet, and gloomy, almost as if something had died.

Looking back now, it was as if it knew the doom that was coming in your absence.

It was a few days after you left that I felt someone shake my leg to wake me up in the middle of the night. I could barely open my eyes. I looked at the dark shadow. It was no nightmare; it was Paaji standing by my bedroom door. The door was half open.

"Come outside," he whispered in Punjabi.

I was so sleepy that I couldn't keep my eyes open. My eyes closed, and I fell back into a deep slumber. I felt someone shaking my leg again. It was Paaji. This time he stood by the right end of my bedside. He was in my room now.

"Come outside," he whispered again.

I looked over from my bed at my older Massi who was sleeping on the bottom bunk bed to my left. I was sleeping on the single bed beside hers and saw her silhouette lying on the bed all tucked in her comforter fast asleep. She did not stir. I was half asleep, but this time, I obeyed. I got up, and Paaji closed the door behind me. He put his arm around me over my shoulders and hugged me close to him so we were side by side. I barely came up to his shoulder. He leaned down and whispered into my ear as he used his arm around my shoulders to push me forward. He guided me along the hallway, past the white metal stairway railing and into the front entry lit by the light coming through the textured yellow glass windows. Finally, we ended up in the living room. I don't remember feeling the carpeted floor beneath me. It was as if the floor too had consented to Paaji and had become a moving walkway. Even the ruffle of my nightgown went quiet as it tapped my ankles.

He walked me toward the L-shaped, crushed velvet green sofa in the living room. It was the beautiful majestic sofa that you, Dad, bought when we first moved into this house. The sofa that had quietly watched me grow and dance for over six years like a loyal respectful spectator. The warm light of the gold lacquered lamp sitting on the center wooden cabinet piece of the sectional sofa hurt my eyes as I tried to open them fully. The TV was on, but I didn't hear any volume.

"You are so nice," Paaji whispered in Punjabi as I squinted.

He sat me on the soft sofa and took a seat right beside me with his arm still around my shoulders. He hugged me. There was an awkward silence in the house; it felt awkward being alone with him in the living room. Something inside me felt uncomfortable and scared. I didn't know what I was afraid of, but I knew I wanted to go back to bed. He cupped my head in both of his hands and moved his hands downwards as if he was fixing my messy hair that I had in two braids.

"You are so beautiful," he said. "You are a good girl. I like you. Come sit on the floor."

He placed both of his hands on my body and moved me from the silent sofa and on to the green shag carpet of the living room floor. It was the same floor I had danced on to countless Bollywood songs, done somersaults and cartwheels on, and had fallen asleep on while waiting for Mom to come home from work. He stood in front of me, facing me with his hands on the sides of each of my shoulders.

"Sit down," he said as the pressure of his hands forced my body down.

I sat down as he kneeled beside me. As soon as I sat down,

Paaji pressed my shoulders backwards until my back was flat against the ground. Something wasn't right. My instincts were going off, telling me to run. I was terrified as he positioned himself by my legs and pulled up my nightgown. I could not comprehend what was going on. It was as if my body knew something horrible was going to happen. I could hear myself making child-like noises—the sounds of a wounded child—as he started peeling off my underwear. In an effort to save myself, I pulled back at my underwear to try and stop him from taking it off. I didn't know what was about to happen. I only knew it wasn't something good.

"No, Paaji. Paaji, don't," I said in Punjabi.

My tiny fingers finally gave way. They were no match against the testosterone rushing through his adult male body. He was over nine years older than me.

I was helpless.

"Kuch nai hunda, kuch nai hunda," he whispered over and over, meaning, *"nothing is going to happen."* Still, he pulled off my underwear. I was so scared, Dad. My body felt paralyzed, frozen, and stiff, as if it was dead. I heard the sound of his zipper open. I remember looking up at the white ceiling with the textured plastered stuff hanging downwards like tiny miniature icicles. Paaji was sitting up with his legs spread apart in a V-position. He pulled my legs apart and positioned himself in the middle. All I could feel was that I was in danger... grave danger.

Unlike in *Star Trek*, there was no protective shield I could call out for that would instantaneously protect me or my body. Captain Kirk would always call out, "All shields up," when he was in danger, and his starship would automatically be protected from enemy attacks. Sometimes he would ask Scotty to beam him up to the starship for safety. But in reality, there was no one for me to call on to beam me away from Paaji. There was no protection for me here.

I saw something between Paaji's legs, something that looked like a dark, thick snake. I held my breath, too afraid to breathe.

He shoved the snake into an entrance in my body—an entrance I didn't know existed yet. My mind and body went numb, and everything around me became super quiet. I didn't feel anything. I didn't hear the ticking of the clock or the usual sound of the fridge going on and off. Time seemed to have stopped. All I could hear was loud silence ringing in my ears. I remained numb on the living room floor. About ten seconds later, he pulled himself away from me, tied up the drawstring to his kacha *(underwear shorts, also known as kachera),* and zipped up his pants.

Dad, the pictures of you, Mom, Uncle and the rest of our family sitting framed on the fireplace mantel all bore witness to what Paaji had done. So did the large images of socialist leaders Karl Marx, Lenin, and Bhagat Singh whom you had framed and hung with pride on the dark brown wood panelled walls. Also present were the two glass dipping birds Mom had bought. Remember, Dad? The ones that wore a hat and were filled with coloured water? The ones that would dip back and forth pretending they were drinking water? Even my favourite green velvet sofa didn't utter a squeak, and the green shag carpet underneath my bare buttocks had lost its lustre. I'm sure in the terror of it all, Mom's vibrant green plants forgot to breathe. The record player sat quietly; its big speakers seemed as if they lost their vibrant disco lights and would remain muted for life.

It all changed in that instant, Dad. Life as I knew it was gone. Little did I know I could never take that moment back again. I couldn't change it, make it right, or make myself perfect. Never!

After Paaji mercilessly invaded my body, he silently put my underwear back on and helped me up. It felt as if I had held my breath through the whole thing. I don't remember breathing, Dad. I kept my head bowed down, my numb mind not able to make any sense of what had just happened. He gave me a hug and whispered something I cannot remember. I quietly walked away from the living room with silence ringing in my ears. As I walked to my bedroom, I could feel something warm trickling down my legs and to my ankles. I crawled into bed, shut off from myself and the world. I closed my eyes and went to sleep. My Massi hadn't moved. Still, there was a little sense of relief knowing I wouldn't get further trouble from her.

Life continued the next day as normal. I told no one what Paaji had done. To be honest, I had no clue what he had done and didn't know how I would even explain in words what happened if I tried. Worst of all, I had know idea what I had lost—what my brother, Paaji, had taken from me. I obeyed him, Dad, just as you had asked. I was a good girl.

It happened again, Dad.

There was a second time. I do not know if it was the next day, the day after that, or the week after.

The third time, Paaji had come home from work. Mom had talked her boss into hiring Paaji for her dishwasher position in the restaurant where she worked while she was away in India. This way, he could earn some money, and Mom could retain her position. He was wearing a blue, mock neck half-sleeve shirt Mom bought him and his dark blue checkered pants he brought from India. His clothes wreaked with all the different smells he brought home with him from work.

Paaji came into my room and woke me up after he had come home from his night shift at work. I obeyed his command to come with him to the living room. Everyone in the house was asleep, including the Massi who had picked him up from work. It was extremely late, around 1:00 a.m., when he laid me on the living room floor closer to the cold fireplace hearth, pulled up my night gown, took off my underwear, unzipped his pants, and lay on top of me. It was hard for me to breathe underneath his weight.

Once again I lay there paralyzed, scared and not remembering to breathe. He was inside me. I didn't utter a word, and I don't remember the mumblings of his whispers. He thrust his hips a few times to finish his business and then got off of me. Like the time before, he pulled up my underwear, helped me up, ran his hands down my head as if smoothing my hair, gave me a hug, and sent me back to my bedroom.

Dad, it happened again and again.

Sometimes it happened more than once a day. If I didn't get up, he would come again and again into my room and shake my leg or foot. I was so scared. The obedient young girl I was always obeyed Paaji's orders. I knew something wrong was going on and if my Massi woke up, I was sure that I would be the one in trouble.

"I like you," Paaji would tell me every day. "You listen and are so nice. You look so beautiful to me. You are so pretty."

He would whisper to me whenever he had a chance. It happened so often that I started getting comfortable with his attentive whispers. Eventually, I even started liking his attention.

Dad, I was raped by your nephew when I was 11 years old.

I had no idea I was raped nor did I keep count how many times it happened in the three months you were gone. But now I know: I was raped, Dad. He would hug me after each time and pull up my underwear before I would hurry back to my bedroom. It became a daily routine in my life, like brushing my teeth, combing my hair, or going to school.

Why did you leave me behind with him, Dad? Through your life's experience, you must have known the threats little girls and women face from men, related to family or not, in our culture. Why did you suspect I would be the one tarnishing your honour? I was only 11. Why did you not put the fear of death into him? Why did you trust him and not me?

When you came back from your trip to India, why did you always scorn me for sitting beside Paaji? Why did you not pull him aside and lay down the law? Why did you not have any rules for him? Why was he a saint to you while I was not even worthy of your trust? I was always so obedient, so why was I so bad?

Because I was born a girl? Because I have a vagina? What more did I have to do? I walked around the house every day like a gutted lamb. I needed you to hold me and help me understand what Paaji was doing to me. I needed you to love and protect me. You were the shepherd who was supposed to protect his sheep. You failed, Dad. You are a traitor, too. You betrayed me, too.

Essentially, it was you who was raped, Dad. You, along with the other adults in the house that Paaji was able to deceive. Without you knowing, he left you marred with shame and bowed in humility. He left you on your knees with slumped shoulders, stripped of family honour with no place to hide. He left you so when the time came for you to find out, the shame wouldn't be able to let you look at yourself in the mirror.

You weren't only betrayed by your nephew, Dad. There were many males along the way who defied your trust: Papa, Pago, Parmar, and Priest. The ultimate betrayal and the hardest for you to bear came from your nephew. You exerted so much energy on being angry, punishing, and yelling at your daughters to ensure Salakshana, Kira, and I were subservient to male authority. You wasted so much of my precious childhood on teaching the three of us obedience that traumatized us for life. I was deathly afraid of you, Dad. You failed to focus on the males around you. You never made known the consequences to them if anyone messed around with your family's honour or your daughter's innocence. You failed to protect your daughter, Dad, because you spent your time breaking down the innocent and powerless instead. You failed to challenge those that held power over your little girls: the males. You always looked at us girls as if we were at fault no matter what happened around the house. Whether it was a dish that broke or milk that spilled, you looked at us as if we were to blame for everything that went slightly wrong. You failed to divert your focus to the true culprits around you. The slithering, slimy snakes, the males, that invaded and wreaked havoc on your family. On me, your innocent little girl.

Look what happened to me because you raised me to be submissive to male authority no matter what. You raised me to live in pain and trauma and believe I didn't matter. You wired my brain in such a way that I believed I was always wrong, unworthy, not good enough, and undeserving of your love. You raised me to suffer in silence. You left me alone, scared, wounded, lost, and confused.

Betrayal is a hard pill to swallow, especially if it's your own family member. I don't blame you, Dad. It's the little girl, the Little Jeeti inside of me, who is angry and upset at you. She still blames you for what Paaji has done.

And now, we both share the betrayal in common, Dad.

With Love,

Jeeti

LETTER 6

It's Okay to Be Confused

Dear Little Jeeti,

The countless daily rapes changed you. You no longer chased butterflies or looked for four leaf clovers in your front yard. No longer did you play with your sisters in the way you once knew. The delight of performing perfect cartwheels with Kira on the green front lawn had become a thing of the past. Without you knowing, your world had changed. Your mind could not keep up with what Paaji was doing to your body, mind, and soul.

Why doesn't he pee in the toilet? Why does he pee inside of me? you would wonder. You thought the warm, runny fluid that he would always leave behind must've been urine. How could you have known what it was when you didn't know anything about the anatomy or biological functions of his body or your own?

It wasn't long before Paaji started to come into your bedroom during the evenings to play cards with you and your sisters, staying late or sneaking in once all the adults were asleep. It was on one of these late nights Paaji told you, "Go warm up my bed downstairs."

His bedroom was in the basement, and during the winter months it was very cold. You, now 12 years old, obeyed. The bed indeed was very cold. You went under the comforter, pulled it up to your chin, curled yourself up to get warm, and slowly went to sleep. When he finally came downstairs, he snuggled against you and raped you.

Another time soon after, he told Salakshana to go warm his bed and said to you, "I have to ask her too so she doesn't suspect anything between us. It is best if both of you alternate." He raped me in my bed upstairs while Salakshana was warming his bed downstairs. Soon after that, he started to lie in your bed between you and Salakshana with the lights out. He would touch your breasts and your vagina. Once Salakshana was asleep, he would pull down your underwear and stick his penis into your vagina.

One day out of the blue, Paaji decided to crawl into Kira's bed.

Why would he do that? you thought. *Her single bed is too tiny to fit a big man and she slobbers a lot when she sleeps.*

As Salakshana lay asleep beside you, you watched him lying in Kira's bed in the dark. You heard the sheets rustle and heard Kira move around seemingly agitated. You wondered what was going on. It was a few weeks after that month when 10-year-old Kira told you something that didn't make sense. You were both downstairs by the boiler room when she told you.

"Paaji put his hand down my pants."

You were completely shocked.

"I am going to tell Dad," she said.

"No, don't tell Dad," you said. You were afraid Dad would punish both you girls, and you thought Paaji must have an explanation. "I will ask Paaji."

"No, don't ask him," she begged. "Promise me you won't ask him."

"I promise," you replied.

Your stomach was queasy and uncomfortable with what she told you. Eventually, you broke your promise to your little sister and asked Paaji.

"It was an accident," he replied, shaking his head. "She is so tiny. I was lying beside her, and I turned over and my hand accidentally touched her."

You believed him. After all, the single bunk bed really was so small, and so was she. In comparison, your body was bigger than hers. She was skinny and flat; your body was changing, becoming much more curvaceous.

Little Jeeti, how confused you were through your preteen years. Your body started developing in ways you couldn't comprehend. The feeble attempt in Grade 7 of sex education did nothing to help you understand what was happening to you. *Intercourse* was too big of a word for you to put into context. The words *penis* and *vagina* were foreign to you, and the simple drawing of each one of them outlined in black did not shed any light. Mom never explained anything to you about the birds and the bees, and neither did your Massis. Salakshana didn't know anything either. No one explained the changes happening to your body. No wonder you were so confused. No one in your household talked about sex while you were growing up. No one talked about how the male and female body worked. Mom, Salakshana, and your Massis hadn't told you anything about a period. When you told one of your Massis there was a dark stain in your underwear, she handed you a white paper towel to tuck between your legs in your underwear. That was it.

The women in your household did not know how to handle your changing body and growing breasts. When one of your Massis told all the other females in the house that you got your period, Salakshana laughed at you. She was also so embarrassed you had developed perky breasts. She would make fun of your breasts that grew bigger and bigger each day. She hid your favourite t-shirt the school librarian had awarded you for helping her over the year after school because she was uncomfortable with how it clung to your breasts. Mom didn't say a word to you about your period. She also didn't notice when you needed a bra. You complained to one of your Massis how your chest hurt when you jogged. It was then Mom gave you an old, worn-out, hand-me-down bra that belonged to your Massis and Salakshana. Your boob would pop out of the A-cup bras because you were a B-cup, quickly becoming a C. One of your Massis started to make snarky comments on your curves. She started pointing out how your stomach stuck out. She even called you fat. Nobody knew what to do with you and your body, including you.

You started to feel shame. You became uncomfortable and embarrassed with your growing breasts and developing thighs. You were constantly told to cover your cleavage, which seemed to show itself no matter how small the neckline of your blouse. You started to hunch your shoulders when you walked in the school hallways, so your large perky breasts wouldn't stick out. You were almost 5'3" and around 122 pounds by Grade 8. You were jogging 2-3 miles a day at times because you now thought you were fat, too. One of your Massis was trying to lose her post pregnancy weight, so you started to follow her diet. You couldn't comprehend why your body was growing and why you couldn't fit into last year's pants no matter how much you dieted or exercised. You had been a very physically active child through elementary school and had participated in numerous sports the school had offered, including cross country running, volleyball, basketball, floor hockey, soccer, and track and field. All the years you had spent in your childhood playing tag, riding your bike, and dancing in your living room didn't seem to make any difference in keeping you slender. You couldn't understand why you were now *fat*.

You were on your own, Little Jeeti. It was left up to you to figure out everything you needed to know about your changing body. I guess Mom thought you would learn all about sex on your wedding night. It wasn't until you were 13 years old, a good year and half after the rapes started, that you decided to look at a library book from your high school to learn how the human body worked. It was a book one of Salakshana's friends had told her about. You started to educate yourself on the male and female body parts and reproductive organs, but still, everything seemed muddled and didn't make sense to you. The book wasn't very explicit.

You were confused, Jeeti, and left to manage Paaji on your own. You had to figure out with your young mind how to fulfill his request of removing your hair from your private area. You didn't know what to use and how it would be safe to do so. Your Massi's Nair cream that she used for her eyebrows? That was a very scary and overwhelming ordeal for you.

Your confusion amplified that summer when Paaji asked you to watch a video that he had hidden high up in the laundry room ceiling. Dad, Uncle, and Paaji would be gone for the weekend to his wrestling tournament in Vancouver.

"Make sure you watch it when no one is home," he had said.

You were doing the dishes that afternoon. Oddly, no one else was home, and you suddenly remembered what Paaji had asked you to do. So, you obeyed. You pressed play on the video player that sat on top of the television set. You took a few steps back from the television to view the screen. It took your brain a few seconds to realize what you were watching. But when you did, you closed your eyes and covered your ears, shocked and horrified by what you saw. You immediately turned it off.

It was pornography, a word you didn't yet know. It was as if an electric shock had gone right through you. Your breathing tripled, and your heart was pounding hard. After a few minutes, with bravery and courage, you pressed the play button once again on the VCR to comply with what Paaji had asked you to do. You became very angry, and your body and hands became hot and sweaty. You were traumatized.

"Did you watch it?" Paaji asked as he held you in his muscular arms when he came back from Vancouver.

You nodded. The video confused you further.

Is that what Paaji is doing to me? you thought. *Am I supposed to enjoy what Paaji is doing to me?*

It was a little while after the video incident when Paaji asked you if you enjoyed what he was doing to you. Embarrassed and uncomfortable, you shook your head firmly to indicate you were not.

He was lying on top of you. Below you was the large wrestling mat Dad had brought into the basement for Paaji. On top of you was the wrestler himself. He was topless, wearing red Adidas sweatpants with white stripes that matched the red wrestling mat and its white circle. He had you locked underneath him. He smelled of sweat. He had been working out, and by now, his muscles had grown. His arms were snuggled around you. You could see the bulge of his biceps on either side of you. His shoulders were big and round, stuffed with rock hard muscles. His chest was solid. Your 13-year-old frame lay still under his firm body.

He asked you again if you enjoyed what he was doing to you, and you repeated the same answer. Then, he asked you a third time. His eyes were full of lust and fiercely locked with yours. His lips were full of an unquenchable thirst and an endless desire. His heart was beating hard against yours. You knew he was looking for a different answer. You could smell the stale, sweaty smell in the air coming from the mat underneath you. You paused momentarily and decided to answer differently so he would stop asking. You immediately took your gaze off of him, moving your head to the side. You were shy, unsure, uncomfortable, and scared.

He used his hand to turn your head back toward him. Your eyes locked into his light eyes. He smiled and was pleased to hear your answer. He was happy.

"Don't be shy," he said as he lay on top of you cupping your face in his one hand. "I love you."

He no longer *liked* you; now, he *loved* you. And he wanted you to say it back to him. So, you did. He told you how beautiful you were and hugged you tight. No man in your life told you these kinds of things. In fact, no one in your family had ever told you they loved you. It made you feel special. You believed him when he said, "This is love, and we are lovers."

It wasn't until after you saw the video that you pieced it all together: Paaji was having sexual intercourse with you. You were having sex. He called it love. You realized you were no longer a virgin.

But he is my cousin, my brother, you thought. You felt you loved him back. You felt conflicted and confused with what was happening and what Paaji was saying to you. You liked this feeling of love. You liked being treated special, hugged and held. You liked the attention you received from him. You had to give in to it because you had no control to stop it. It was not possible for you to go back and undo everything. It felt too dangerous and unsafe to tell someone.

You started to feel shame and see yourself as a soiled and dirty little girl. There was no place for the likes of you in your family or in the world. You had seen it countless times in Bollywood movies, although it didn't make sense to you at the time. The women in the Bollywood movies would be so devastated when they had their sari pulled off, blouse torn, and bindi smeared. They would be screaming and crying as they ran away from the men. The women would then be ousted from the family and village because they were no longer pure. They were blamed and considered trash. She had been raped, but you didn't know it then.

It all made sense to you now. You understood why those women wanted to end their lives. You knew that their virginity and honour were stolen. They were no longer pure, and no man would ever want to marry them. Death was the only option for any woman who suffered this fate. In the movies, they would end their lives by standing in front of a train, jumping off a cliff, drowning themselves in a river, slitting their wrists, or drinking poison. They thought they did not deserve to live because they were dirty and dishonoured. No man would ever want them now.

Daily incidents occurring around you in the real world reinforced what lay in store for you if anyone ever found out what Paaji was doing to you. Your cousin in Vancouver was only 14 years old when she was forced to marry someone in India. Mom and Dad had said she was "kharab" or "bigad gai" *(meaning bad, gone bad, or has done wrong)*. She wasn't obeying her parents and was going out with boys, so her parents took her to India and married her off.

A 15-year-old girl in your neighbourhood had suffered the same fate. Her parents also took her to India, married her off, and confiscated her Canadian passport. It was about a year later when they finally allowed her back into Canada. Another high school girl in the community was forcibly arranged to be married overnight at 4:00 a.m. because her family did not approve of the boy she wanted to marry from our hometown.

You heard many stories of daughters who were disowned or shipped off to India as you were growing up. It was your reality. You were frightened because you knew full well that you would be shipped off and married as a child bride or possibly even killed in India. You truly believed your head would be chopped off. You knew you were to blame for what Paaji was doing to you. The women in the Bollywood movies were always shamed and never believed. The girls being shipped off to India were always to blame. They were an example of what happens to girls who did not obey and disgraced the family honour. They were an example you did not want to replicate.

You had to believe what Paaji was telling you. You had to believe how much he loved you, how beautiful you were, what a good girl you were, and how special you were.

"I love you," he told you every day. "I wish I could buy you from your dad. I would give him $100,000 for you. If we were Muslims, we could get married. Pakistani people are allowed to marry their cousins."

You were scared, Jeeti, of everything. You always had late periods, and he would ask you to eat halon *(aserio)* seeds thinking it stopped pregnancy. He also asked you to take your Massi's birth control pills. You looked at the round dial container and had no idea which one to take. The one on the left or the one on the right of the dial? You took one, and it made you feel sick and nauseous all day. You never took it again, despite his badgering. You were scared your Massi would find out, and the sick feeling the pill gave you was unbearable. Thank goodness the Almighty had taken care of certain aspects of his biology.

Culturally, all you knew was that a woman belonged to only one man in her lifetime. She only shared her body with one man, and for you, that man had to be Paaji, the one who took your virginity. You obeyed him and were powerless in front of his demands. You accepted what Paaji was doing to you. You accepted that it was love. You accepted the attention he gave you. You accepted you were special to him. You believed that you were lovers because you had to believe it. It was the only way you could make sense of it all.

And you knew now that you would have to kill yourself one day.

You would have to kill yourself so your parents wouldn't marry you to someone else. Mom and Dad would want to marry you off one day, and you couldn't let that happen. You would have no way to explain why you weren't a virgin to your future husband. You were better off being dead than ever trying to explain why you weren't a virgin. At such a young age, you figured out you were doomed, and only death would be an option for you. Paaji had taken your virginity, and from what you understood, you had to be loyal to the man who took your virginity. You understood a girl could only love one man. You thought you could not love another man—that you belonged only to Paaji.

How messed up and confused you were! You thought you had a hand in what Paaji was doing to you. You thought it was you who participated in a sinful act every day. You thought you were to blame for what he was doing to you. You thought it was you who had crossed the boundaries of a brother and sister relationship. You were so indoctrinated that you thought you bore all the blame and shame. You knew you had no control over your own life. You never wanted anyone to say anything bad about Paaji and worried what would happen to him if anyone ever found out.

Sweet Little Jeeti, ever since you were a little girl, it warmed your heart to see love in the movies. Your heart always filled with tenderness when you saw Bollywood actors dancing and singing love songs to the shy, timid actresses. You loved when Clint Eastwood fell in love with a Southern belle or when Elvis Presley looked into the eyes of his lover. You always thought you would find true love, be married, and have a family one day. But contrary to what you had seen in the movies, there would be no Romeo or Ranja in your life. Kismet had decided you belonged to Paaji. Your dreams of one day marrying a handsome prince and dancing in the luscious fields with your love, adorned in your Indian jewels, and ghagra choli, and singing your favourite Bollywood melody, were shattered.

You tried to do the best you could to survive day by day. Despite what was happening to you, you made moments filled with laughter and joy. You weren't depressed and miserable. You loved having fun and usually smiled and laughed a lot. You loved to play sports at high school, too, and you loved to dance and play games at home.

You loved having your cousin Joe from Vancouver over for the Christmas holidays. He too loved coming over; it gave him a good sense of family, love, and belonging. He also loved how you all bonded as family and were fun to be around. You and all your siblings loved to play with this fun, mischievous, raised-in-the-city cousin. Paaji was always grumpy when this particular cousin came over. He did not like you playing or giving any attention to him. Paaji was very disappointed in you if you sat beside this cousin and would punish you by giving you the silent treatment, ignoring you, and being cold toward you. He scorned if this cousin ever leaned on top of you or sat beside you.

You did not like disappointing Paaji. It was hard for you to please him. Once when he was upset at you, you took a piece of wire, bent it into an "M" shape, heated it up on the stove, and placed it against your chest to show him you were obedient. The mark soon faded, but the need to be obedient to Paaji didn't.

Many times it seemed impossible to please him. No matter what you did, it was never enough.

Numerous times, when Paaji would be gravely disappointed in you, you would lock yourself in the washroom, open the left mirrored cabinet that stored Uncle's toiletries, and reach for his silver Gillette safety razor. It had a 4-inch silver round handle with a flat top casing that took a flat 1-3/4 x 3/4 inch sharp double edge blade. With a certain determination and numbness, you would unscrew the old school razor blade cover and take out the razor from its shell. You would hold the blade in your hand and try to slit your wrist. The actresses in the Bollywood movies made it look way too easy. Your tears blurred your vision as you tried. You wiped your tears and continued to complete your mission. It was too painful for you to cut through your flesh, deep into the tissue and then into the vein. When you didn't succeed on the right side, you would attempt the other wrist. The sharp blade would knick the fingers of your left hand just like it had when you were little and Dad angrily made you remove the nail polish you and your sister wore with his razor blade. You had cried back then too as the blade cut your tiny fingers repeatedly and cut through your nail bed as the blood oozed out. You cried now too every time you tried to make a cut and then cursed yourself for not being able to succeed. You were feeling so much despair and hopelessness. You were so alone in confused darkness.

You didn't know what else to do.

One day Kira, who was 11 years old at the time, caught you. You were lying in your bedroom on her single bunk bed with your left hand outside of the comforter. She noticed blood on your wrist as you lay on your left side sobbing in bed. It was Christmas, and your cousin Joe was visiting for the holidays. You had extremely disappointed Paaji, but you didn't know why.

"I'm going to tell Mom," she said.

"No, no, no," you begged her, "please don't tell Mom."

"Promise me you will never do it again," she said.

You promised, and you kept your promise.

But brave Little Jeeti, you knew full well one day the day would come where you would have to die. The record played deep in your subconscious. Thoughts of having to kill yourself came in and out of your mind as they pleased. The record of death played in silence in your subconscious on repeat.

The women in Bollywood films sometimes threw themselves in front of trains, so you started considering where the nearest tracks were. You often heard the train go by during the day, but you had never been down to the tracks. You thought through in your mind exactly how to get to the tracks. From your house you could see the beautiful scenic mountain where you knew the train passed by. You wondered if your mind would be in the same zone as the Bollywood actress who walked down the train tracks, numb and deaf to the sound of the train approaching, or if you would jump away once the train got close. You imagined what the moment would be like when the train would hit you.

Another time, when you were on your Grade 8 science field trip, you looked into the river and thought, *This is a good place to die. I have to remember how to get here.* The Fraser River was flowing so fast, it would have no problem engulfing you. You imagined it carrying you away easily and effortlessly. You thought about what your family would think after you were dead. Would they miss you? Would they understand why? Would they still love you?

Despite the darkness that surrounded you during your teenage years, you still loved to dance and emulate Bollywood actresses. You would crank up the music and dance daily to their tunes. You danced in your imaginary world, visiting spectacular places only seen in the Bollywood world. Your love for fabrics and design was born and flourished solely because of the Bollywood world. At such a young age, you embraced sewing, perfecting your skill with every ensemble. Your imagination was boundless, your creativity soared, and your ability to design was impeccable.

You would lay down a khesi on the living room carpet, gather your measuring tape, home made pattern, pen marker, pins, and silk fabric, and put them on the khesi. You had learned from Mom to use the khesi as your cutting table. You would measure and mark the silk and then cut into the vibrant fabric with confidence and delight. You loved the sound of the scissors cutting into silk. Sometimes your legs would fall asleep as you sat and completed your cutting, but you did not care. You would shuffle from one leg to another, immersed in complete joy and excited to finish the first phase of your ensemble. Indian clothing was not available to purchase off the rack back then, so you delighted in creating your own salwar kameez *(traditional Punjabi long top with loose pants)*.

You were so vibrant and confident in many ways, Little Jeeti, especially in your dancing. At this age you were mesmerized by Rekha. You watched her intensely as she danced with utmost grace. You practiced how she moved and learned how to swivel your hips just like her. You danced just like Rekha. You also learned how to do Bhangra by watching Punjabi movies. You were a natural. Dancing brought you so much joy, made you so alive, and always took you to an electrifying, free, imaginary place. You were so beautiful and radiant that you illuminated the darkness around you and others. No one could see the tormenting storm that would come and go inside you. Something about you glowed despite your internal despair.

On the outside, you were unique, eclectic, and different. Your friends at school admired you, you were a lot of fun to have around, your sisters loved you, and your family cared for you.

To the world, you were the perfect, beautiful child.

But deep inside your being, you knew how imperfect and impure you were.

You must realize one thing, virtuous Little Jeeti: There was nothing you could have done to remain pristine. The instant your innocence, your virginity, was snatched from you without you knowing, you were branded guilty. Guilty of losing your honour, shaming your family, and becoming a disgrace. If you had opened your mouth or cried out for help, you would have been blamed for not being able to keep your virginity. You would have been accused of wanting it. The adults around you would not have believed you, nor would they have comprehended the fact you truly had nothing to do with it. The onus was on you, little girl, to protect what is the most sacred gem for a woman. The onus was on you to protect the honour of your family, no matter what your age.

How were you supposed to know that at such a tiny age? How were you to know you had something to protect? Something deemed pure and priceless? Something called virginity? Something you didn't know existed until it was already gone?

Why would something so treasured come without a lock or its own alarm system? How were you to know your honour and your family's honour rested between your legs? How could you be carrying something so valuable and precious without anyone telling you about its significance, purpose, and existence? How could you hold the burden of an entire family? An entire culture?

It wouldn't have mattered when you opened your mouth, Little Jeeti. The reality was, you would have been branded a liar. You would have been blamed regardless of Paaji's actions. It was you who would have been punished. He and the other pedophiles took advantage of that through the course of your childhood.

They, especially Paaji, knew the blame would entirely lie on you.

With Love,

Jeeti

LETTER 7

You Are Still Beautiful

Dear Little Jeeti,

Growing up, you were always told how beautiful you were.

You had big, brown eyes that were accented with perfect eyebrows, long, dark brown silky hair, pink lips, and a perfect princess nose. You looked beautiful in your innocence. It was your summer school teachers when you were a child who you remember first discussing your beauty. Then it was the women at the gurdwara who would tell your Mom how beautiful you were. Many times when you would go to someone's house, the Aunty, or the lady of the house, would comment on how pretty you were. You always shied away from the attention and flattery. As much as it felt good that you were beautiful, it made you uncomfortable because you didn't know what to do or say. You would smile, bow your head, keep quiet, hide behind your Mom, and shy away.

When Mom was pregnant with your brother, Jesse, she would come into your room to wake you and Salakshana up for school. If Salakshana got up first and said good morning to her, Mom would get mad and say she wanted to see your face first instead. In Indian culture, many believe that when you are pregnant, you should always look at a beautiful face so your baby would be beautiful too. The first face you see in the morning, that's what the baby would look like.

Hearing praise about your beauty from adults added to your confidence and self assurance. Your confidence soared daily throughout your childhood years as you visualized and imagined yourself to be as beautiful as the Bollywood actresses. You felt beautiful not only on the outside, but in many ways on the inside too, despite the ugliness around you. You felt a specialness that existed about you. You loved the special attention Paaji gave you. You drank every loving word and kind phrase he said to you, not realizing they were poison. Your stomach would flutter with excitement when he hugged you and told you how beautiful you were or how much he loved you. Every day you drank the verbal potion he had concocted just for you without question.

But the horrific incidents that occurred with Paaji chipped away at how you felt about yourself inside. You didn't have the power to stop him. When you said, "No," he never took it for an answer. He didn't listen to your pleas to stop when you were deathly afraid someone would walk in on you both, especially Papa who you thought suspected something. You didn't tell him when you didn't like it or if it hurt. You felt as if you were performing some duty for him and couldn't question it. It was your duty as a good girl, as a lover. Many times you would feel shame and disgust with yourself and with what Paaji was doing to you.

Yet somehow, there was a spark, a beautiful flame that danced and burned inside you. You would dance and become one with this flame and feel its beauty as the vibrations of the Bollywood music increased the height and flicker of this flame. Its magical glow kept lit a fire in you so your inner beauty would never burn out, die, or be extinguished by anyone, not even Paaji and the odour he left behind.

You went to school every day despite the odour that came from you. It was the stinky smell of semen that would never go away, even if you changed your underwear. By the time you reached school, your underwear would be soiled again with semen that dripped from your vagina without any care for you. The smell would not go away no matter how tightly you kept your legs closed. You would get whiffs of it as you moved one classroom to another and even during gym. You wondered if anyone else could smell him on you. The smell was a constant reminder of the darkness that lurked around you no matter where you went.

Beautiful Little Jeeti, you were then around 14 years old with a desire to do really well in school. The dark ugliness made a home in your life, all around you day and night. It followed you everywhere like a shadow. There was no escaping it. It became an unwelcome guest. An intruder you learned to live with. An intruder no one else saw except you.

It accompanied you that day when you stood outside on your back sundeck holding a large kitchen knife in your hand. It was the knife Uncle used to use to cut off the head of the large, two-foot salmon and filet it. You were looking far off West into the beautiful hills where the train always passed by the green pastures surrounded by trees. It was the place with the pasture of green grass in which you wished one day you could jump into and dance for real. You had always wondered what it would be like to live out there. That day, in your mind, you played the sound the blade used to make against the knife sharpener every time Uncle sharpened it. Your right elbow rested on the white wooden railing while your hand held the knife horizontally, swinging it back and forth toward your throat. Each time you felt the sharp cold blade against your neck, you were wishing it would somehow slit your throat on its own.

You wished you were dead.

Despite those dark days, you still found moments of light. You were still a little girl, after all. During these dark days, it was your beauty that lit your path of daily survival. I'm not referring to the outer beauty that you saw in the mirror daily; it was your inner beauty. It was that beautiful, luminous spark inside that kept you alive and thriving as a teenager. It was your inner beauty that allowed you to wash away the disgust from the outside and inside of your body—from the repugnant smell of runny nasty semen that had become your daily perfume. It was your inner beauty that allowed you to feel joy and bathe in sparks of light that washed away the darkness. It was this inner beauty that allowed you to create many memorable moments of joy, like the samosa and chai Indian dance parties you had at home with your sisters and female friends. Phenji Phenji parties is what you liked to call them *(Phenji meaning sister).*

The inner beauty came from you, Little Jeeti. It was the part of you that knew only how to love and give love. You gave unconditional love to your sisters, brother, family, cousins, friends, teachers, guests, aunts, and uncles. You gave love to those that verbally and sexually abused you, including Paaji. It was your deep belief in love and ability to give authentic love that allowed your inner beauty to shine and radiate in the Pooni household and the lives of others. It was your ability to give genuine love no matter what was going on that allowed you to dive deep into your imagination, your passion to create, and your desire to be bold and beautiful. It was your ability to love that enabled you to uphold family values dear to your heart—values of trust, loyalty, kindness, and compassion. All this combined amplified your inner beauty and that illuminated your outer beauty. Your inner beauty was much more important than your outer beauty.

You were only beautiful on the outside because you were so beautiful on the inside.

Yes, you despised yourself many times through your dark young teenage years. The cackle in your head that reminded you of being a huge disgrace and shame to your family shadowed your mind periodically.

How could you?
How could you be sleeping with your own brother?

How could you be in love with your own brother?
Are you stupid?
You are such a disgrace. What will Mom think of you?
What will your sisters think of you?
What will all those that love you think of you?
You know what Dad will do to you if he ever finds out.
Everyone thinks you are a good girl; you are no good.
Wait until your friends find out how rotten you are.
How can you live with yourself?
You are not pure. You are not a virgin. You didn't keep your virginity.
You can never get married.
Poor Mom and Dad, what are they going to do with you?
You are disgusting. You are rotten.

You were more worried about what would happen to him. You didn't want anyone to hate him.

Yet miraculously, you were able to bathe yourself in the tiniest speck of self love that existed inside you, and you allowed the spark of your inner beauty to stay alive rather than diminish under the gusting storm Paaji brought into your life. You, Little Jeeti, were able to tap into your soul beauty, so when feelings of ugliness came upon you, they only lasted a day or so. Soul beauty, your own encryption inscribed within you at conception, was yours alone. There was no power that could take away, alter, or delete it. The nasty feelings weren't able to abolish or destroy you. Your soul sang its own song and its own rhythm that you danced to endlessly, gleaming in its sacred light. Your internal flame of love, life, and beauty flickered and threatened to diminish but never gave way to the puffs of deep dark despair.

Like the sweet smell of incense, it was your inner soul beauty that scented the Pooni household.

With Love,

Jeeti

LETTER 8

You Will Be Taken Advantage Of

Dear Little Jeeti,

They left as they came, one by one.

All the relatives Mom and Dad helped sponsor from India and opened their home, their wallets, and their hearts to began to leave. For years they had given them beds to sleep on, comforters to keep them warm, delicious food to fill their bellies, and education in how to settle in this new country. They helped them find jobs, taught them how to drive, and showed them the importance of learning English. They gave them confidence. They provided emotional and financial support.

But the most important thing Mom and Dad gave them was genuine love, as if they were their parents. Love that was unconditional. Love that helped these immigrants survive. They also gave them power over you and your siblings, allowing them to have free rein to discipline all of you as they wished. Instead you were told to give your relatives love and treat them with respect. You had to obey them, especially the males. Salakshana, Kira, and you had to share your tiny little room with your three Massis until they married and their husbands arrived. You had to sleep with the meanest Massi. For years, you were six people in one tiny room sleeping on three small single beds with no room for privacy, let alone opening the closet. At one point there were 15 family members living in your house. You opened up your heart to these people and gave them love, following your parent's footsteps.

They all took from Mom and Dad, and they all took shamelessly and freely to their heart's content, as if Mom and Dad owed it to them. Mom and Dad gave and gave selflessly, expecting nothing in return. It gave them joy and a sense of fulfillment to help out their family members. Mom and Dad had fulfilled their duties of helping their extended families leave poverty and have better, more prosperous lives. When these relatives had first come into your home from India, they looked like toothpicks. When they left your home in Williams Lake and moved to Edmonton, they had meat on their bodies and were very healthy. They also knew Mom and Dad would be there for them financially whenever they needed. What a great cushion to have! Mom and Dad were great mentors for these people. They were a great older brother and sister to them all; in a sense, they were a great mother and father to them all.

During this whole time, Salakshana, Kira, Jesse, Rakhee, and you got lost in the shuffle. Mom and Dad had given all their attention to their relatives; they were too busy helping others, fulfilling their obligations to their extended families and work, to notice us. They failed to keep a connection with their own children and foster good communication and understanding with each one. You don't ever remember Mom hugging you as a child, sitting you in her lap and giving you affection. She was too busy. Dad never spent much time with you either. The only time he said anything to you or your sisters was when he was disappointed or angry at you girls. Both Mom, Dad, and the adults in the house ignored the red flags that indicated something was happening between you and Paaji. In fact, when you were around 13 years old, Mom told you Dad had asked her to tell you not to sit close to Paaji. Dad had said, "The boy is good; it's your daughter that's bad. She is the one who sits too close to him."

Mom and Dad were distracted with the daily chaos in the house, and that distraction enabled them to make another choice they would one day come to regret: marrying off Salakshana at 19 to a man in India who was older than her.

They themselves didn't travel to India to see who he was, what he looked like, how he behaved, how he lived, or what life views he held. They trusted the words of a family friend, the middlewoman, that he would be a good suitor. Mom was fixated on one thing.

"He doesn't have a large family, only an older sister in England, which means Salakshana would never have to deal with in-laws," she said.

Mom and Dad knew how hard life could be for an Indian girl with a large family of in-laws. This man had no parents, so it was just him that would be coming to Canada. That was enough to convince Mom he was a good match for Salakshana. Mom, Dad, your aunts, and your uncles always referred to Salakshana as "Bholi," meaning naive. You had heard that ever since you could remember. They thought she wasn't smart enough, wasn't pretty enough, and wasn't tall enough. They saw her as too naive to understand the ways of life. Mom and Dad knew their naive daughter wouldn't be able to handle the pettiness, drama, and pressure of any in-laws, especially an Indian mother-in-law.

You couldn't understand how your sister was to marry a complete stranger. You felt uncomfortable for her. You had seen arranged marriages time and time again in Bollywood movies, but when it came to your sister, you weren't happy inside. The man's black and white picture looked nothing like the handsome actors in the Bollywood movies. He wore a turban, had a full beard, and looked much older than your sister. He was a non-practicing Sikh Punjabi and of the same caste. (Mom and Dad always stated we could not marry out of caste.) He looked nothing like your clean shaven, handsome Dad. You felt fear inside for yourself, knowing one day it would be your turn. As the second oldest, you were next in line to finish high school, and Mom and Dad had arranged marriages in mind for their daughters right after graduation. As per Indian tradition, that was the norm. Yours too would be an arranged marriage, of course, since girls were strictly forbidden to date and not allowed to have boyfriends back then.

Marriage—a legal or formally recognized union of two people as partners in a personal relationship.

You could not see yourself in a union with anyone. Life had already formally dictated a union for you—a union with Paaji. What Paaji was doing and saying to you every day solidified that union. In your young mind, you understood he was the only one you could ever be with. You were not worthy of having anything else. Nothing could change that.

You were 15 years old that sad day in March 1984 when you watched your older sister marry a man she hadn't seen. A man she didn't know. A man who knew nothing about Canadian culture. A man who had twisted views about girls raised in Canada.

"Girls in Canada are bad," he whispered loudly to you when he and Salakshana came back a week later to visit Williams Lake.

You and Kira had to give up your bedroom to the newlyweds and were told to sleep on the sofa in the living room. By 9:30 p.m., the adults in the house had all gone to bed. Your brother-in-law came into the living room and sat on the sofa chair. You were lying on the sofa beside the chair, and Kira was lying on the opposite side. You were surprised and found it odd he was up and out of the bedroom since all the other adults had gone to bed. You were shy around him and didn't converse with him. You didn't know him. He was a complete stranger who was now a part of your family.

He sat on the chair and watched TV for a few minutes, and then Salakshana, my newlywed sister, decided to join us. She sat on the living room floor facing the TV with her back toward us. As she watched TV, he started talking.

"She doesn't trust you and me," he said in a low voice, speaking in Punjabi. "That is why she came out of the room and is not in bed. Adhering to the rule of your Indian culture where every male is either your brother or uncle, you gave your brother-in-law the title of brother, Paaji, and the respect and trust that comes along with it."

"Paaji? My sister is not like that," you replied in Punjabi.

Salakshana turned around and looked over at us innocently.

"See that is why she is turning around to look at us. To see what we are doing. She doesn't trust you and me," he said adamantly.

"My sister is not like that," you repeated with courage. "You shouldn't say that about her."

You were uncomfortable with what he was saying and had no clue why he would say something like that.

The man continued his nonsense talk. "Do you think about having sex?"

You were stunned. Not knowing what to say to your brother-in-law or how to handle the conversation you said, "Paaji?"

You were disgusted. You looked over at Kira and tried to sink deep into the sofa, wishing he would go away.

"Do you feel like having sex?" he continued.

"NO!" you said curtly in disgust, hoping he would shut up.

"Do you use your fingers? Do you insert them into your vagina?" he continued shamelessly.

You were repulsed and shocked by what this new Paaji was asking you. Your 15-year-old-mind did not know what to do. You just wanted him to shut up.

"Girls in Canada are bad," he said. "They do it with a broomstick."

"Girls in Canada aren't like that," you replied, disgusted to your core.

Hoping to put an end to the appalling conversation, you got up and sat straight on the sofa, putting more distance between you and him and sending him a message to shut up and stay away. He was now further from your ear and would need to talk even louder. To protect yourself, you drew your blanket close around your neck and shoulders. You looked over at Kira, and she was looking directly at you. Your body shuddered as your mind was trying to deal with what this new, trusted "brother" of yours had just asked you. Unable to comprehend the horror that had just passed, you sat quietly pretending to watch TV. You were so scared, shaking inside wishing he would leave.

Soon, he got up and went to bed. Salakshana followed him a little while later. You were so glad she stayed up longer than him and that she did not leave you and Kira alone with him.

It was later that you, Mom, and all your Massis learned of the nightmare he had put Salakshana through on her wedding night. The nightmare actually started as soon as she was given away from your parent's house, right when she sat beside him in the back seat of the decorated wedding car.

"You better bleed," were some of his first words to her.

It was a long three and a half hour car ride for her to the town he was taking her to. On that wedding night, immediately after having intercourse with his new bride that he didn't know at all, he turned on the lights and checked the bed sheet for blood stains; there wasn't any. He degraded her verbally and was more concerned about what he would tell his male relatives. He told her she was a slut, that she wasn't beautiful, that she wasn't pretty. He boasted how he had only married her to come to Canada. He rejected her and the love she would have given him as a wife on their first night of marriage.

It was uncomfortable and weird for you to listen to Mom, your two Massis, and him having a discussion about how your older sister did not bleed virgin blood. Mom came up with reasons to explain why, educating him about tampons used for periods and the insertion of medication to treat vaginal yeast infections. Fear rose inside you as you listened to the adults talk. The conversation reminded you how important it was to be a virgin and to show it in blood. You knew you were next in line to marry, and you would have to go through the same ordeal as Salakshana when your parents married you off. You felt powerless and knew you would avoid marriage at all costs. You could never marry.

Your sweet, naive, innocent sister. What had she married? What had Mom and Dad done? They did not see they were being taken advantage of and so were their daughters. How could they? They were oblivious all these years to the one who had taken the most advantage of them and the entire Pooni family: your cousin, Paaji. The one who used a divide and conquer strategy to separate you sisters. The one who called Kira a kuti *(bitch)* and told you how he didn't like her. The one who told you how ugly Salakshana looked when she was eating mango. The one who had laid ownership to the body, mind, and heart of one of Mom and Dad's good daughters, stripping her of her identity and encasing her in a new one weaved by him. One that revolved around him and only him.

That daughter was you, Little Jeeti.

With Love,

Jeeti

LETTER 9

You Were Immaculately Groomed

Dear Young Jeeti,

"I don't want to get married. I don't want to marry her," you heard Paaji say over and over again.

"Then don't," you said, feeling the pain and angst in your heart.

"My parents want me to," he replied.

His parents had arranged his wedding to a girl from India. He received a picture of her from India.

"If you don't want to marry her, then tell your parents," you said. "Tell your brother, tell your sister, tell someone."

You couldn't understand why he would marry someone if he didn't want to. He was a man. Men had power. He could say no. Deep inside, you wanted him to say no. There were many questions left unanswered.

What were you supposed to do?
What would happen to you?
Where would your place be in his life?
Where would you belong?
Where would you go?

You had graduated high school and were living in Edmonton with one of your Massis, Mom's middle sister, who was married to Dad's nephew, Paaji's older brother. This was the same Massi and Masser who had moved out of your home in Williams Lake back in 1982. Paaji was Masser's younger brother, and he lived with them, too. It was a joint family household. Salakshana had moved in with them a year earlier along with her husband and baby girl, your niece Chandani. To pursue post-secondary education, your parents would only allow you to live with family. A small town Indian girl living on her own was unfathomable to your parents and not widely accepted in Indian culture. Paying for your education was all they could handle. Extra expenses of high rent and bills were out of the question. You were fortunate Dad allowed you to study further after high school; it wasn't the norm culturally. Because of Salakshana's marriage troubles, they didn't bring up any talk of marrying you off right out of high school.

Mom and Dad had first sent you to live with your Phua and her family in Vancouver to pursue your education, but you only lasted there four months. You couldn't handle the drama and dysfunction of that family, and you didn't feel you belonged in Vancouver. You asked Mom if you could move to Edmonton and were ecstatic when she finally agreed. You were very close with Masser and had a lot of love and respect for him. Your sister and niece were there, and of course, Paaji was there, too.

Even though Paaji had moved away to Edmonton from your home in Williams Lake a year earlier, his hold on you never faded. In his absence, it had only grown stronger. Talking to him on the phone once a month or seeing him once a year on a family vacation to Edmonton was not enough to settle the uneasiness and separation you felt without him. Once you moved, Phua, who had suspected something about you and Paaji, made accusations that got you in a whole lot of trouble from your Dad and Uncle. The matter, for the time being, was put to rest when Masser, who had believed this couldn't possibly be true, was able to convince them otherwise. Perhaps it was easier for everyone to turn a blind eye.

Paaji married in October 1987 when he was 27 years old. You were 18 at the time and enrolled at Grant MacEwan College in Edmonton, where you were studying economics. It was no secret to Paaji or yourself that one day he would marry. You both knew that day would come one day, and then suddenly, that day was here.

October came without any care for the disturbance in the house, bringing along with it cold and ruthless darkness. There was so much turmoil inside and around you. The months leading up to Paaji's October wedding were unbearable. Your heart was sinking, with each pump drowning in its own misery. The highs you had felt since you were 11 whenever Paaji had praised you and told you how much he loved you now became your deepest lows, touching the bottom depths of the ocean of sorrow. It was as if something inside you was dying. You were restless. You couldn't eat. An order of a small basket of fries at the cafeteria in the afternoon was your breakfast, lunch, and dinner. Even that felt like too much for your stomach to handle. You couldn't think. You couldn't settle your insides and soothe yourself. You didn't know what to do, where to go, or where you belonged. As a result of what must have been high anxiety, you lost weight, dropping down many sizes so that you could fit into Kira's jeans.

When you were home, you wanted to go to college. When you arrived at the college campus, you wanted to go back home. You would stare out the window on the bus ride to and from home, yet you saw nothing. No outside buildings, neighbourhoods, or people. Everything around you was all a big blur. One day blended into the next with the same constant uneasiness eating at your core. No matter where you went, you weren't settled. You were so lost inside, feeling numb and isolated. You were walking around as if you were a wounded, abandoned nomad. It was as if you were dead.

The torture was unbearable. No one knew what you were going through. No one saw your tears, heartache, and pain. No one smelled you decaying and rotting from the inside out. Those around you saw you as normal, but you were far from it at that point. The October days grew even colder, shorter, and gloomier. You thought the way you knew life with Paaji was over and so were all the years of his promises of love. This was the end—the end of you and him. You would forever be alone. A loner who would never be able to tell anyone why. A loner who knew not who she was, how she would survive, or what she was supposed to do.

Paaji was gone for a week. The wedding was to take place far away in a town on the island off the coast of British Columbia. Masser didn't want to take too many people to the wedding, so only four members from your Edmonton family left for the wedding: Masser, Paaji, and their mom and dad. Thank goodness you didn't have to go. You didn't know how you would have survived through it all. Even though Salakshana and other family members were around you, you felt so alone.

It was such a painful time for you, and it felt as if the pain would never go away. Not knowing how to deal with the pain made it harder. You tried to ignore the painful throbbing of your heart and your senseless world. You were broken. So broken not even the finest silk thread in the world would ever be able to sew you back up again. No amount of mending would be enough to put the pieces of your heart back together. Many days you cried quietly in bed to release the pain. You prepared yourself to accept his marriage, his wife, and the unknown that would come next for you. You had no choice. She would belong to him now and he to her. There would be no place for you in Paaji's life.

If he truly loved me as much as he said all these years, he wouldn't have gotten married, you thought.

It was late evening a week later when Paaji and those who went with him came back with the new bride. It was so awkward. You brushed away the awkwardness and greeted his new wife, too. You all sat around in the living room. One by one the members of the house, including the new bride, went to bed. Paaji stayed up. He would not go to his room.

"Go to your room," you told him. "Your wife is waiting for you."

He would not go upstairs. Instead he sat beside you.

"I love you," he said repeatedly.

He would not leave you alone. He said he wanted to be with you. You sat there, lifeless, completely empty, hollow, and tattered. He wanted to do things to you, to your body. He made that face with glazed eyes. It was the face he had always made when you were a child. The face you first saw when you were 11 years old.

You warded off his advances. He whispered repeatedly into your ear how much he loved and wanted to be with you. He tried to kiss you again and again. You wanted him to leave you alone. You felt so helpless and confused. Your brain was mush and filled with fog. All of its signals and circuits were shut off. It didn't seem it would ever turn on again. Your body was numb. His kisses along your neck that once sent tingles stirred nothing but more emptiness in the vast desert of loneliness and confusion. The more you tried to push him away, the more persistent he became.

"You should go," you said. "You are going to get in trouble."

"I don't care," he said.

"What will your wife think? Please go," you begged.

He did not care. The night wore on, the hours ticked by, and Paaji's advances did not end. Before you knew it, it was close to 5:00 am. Soon members of the house would be up. If anyone saw Paaji with you at that hour, it would mean big time trouble. He was supposed to be with his wife. Your insides started racing, and you could feel the uneasiness inside you grow. You could feel the fear crawling into you. It was as if your inside was telling you that you were in danger.

One voice inside of you was crying out, *"Get it over with, and Paaji will leave you alone."* The other voice was crying just as loudly, *"No, no, no!"*

Your brain started firing overwhelming signals left and right, as if it was having a ping pong match in panic mode. Everything about what was right and wrong—what you should do—became a big jumble. You felt powerless. No matter what you did, it would never be right. Chaos, uncertainty, and confusion consumed every bit of you, as if there was no you left in you. You felt like an empty shell. You were exhausted. Every bit of your insides had crumbled as Paaji became more adamant and desperate as the clock ticked on.

Finally, you caved into his demands. What he was about to do was wrong. What you were about to let him do was wrong. There was just no power left in you to stop him. It was as if you did not own yourself, your body, your heart, and your worthiness. He owned it all. He held the deed. It was as if a more powerful force was at play—a force you could not reason with, talk to, plead with, or beg. It overrode your brain. It felt like you had no choice but to bow to that force. It was as if Paaji was the snake charmer and you the obedient snake who always swayed to the mesmerizing tune of your charmer's flute.

He held your hand and led you into the dining room. It was a small basic room across from the kitchen. Faint light seeped in from the kitchen and dining room window fading away the darkness so you could see. The dining room walls were basically bare. All the lights in the house were off. The dinner table was pushed against one wall with the chairs around it. The tablecloth was covered in plastic. You could feel the cold plastic of the chair as he bent you over, just as he had done numerous times over the exercise bench in the laundry room in Williams Lake when you were 13. In a few seconds, he was done. He hugged you and smoothed your hair just like he had done when you were a little girl. He told you how much he loved you and what you meant to him. Then, he went off to bed. You could hear him go upstairs one stair at a time. You heard his bedroom door open and close. Your insides fell to the floor.

It wasn't supposed to be this way.

There was a part of you that was upset at yourself and upset at Paaji. There was another part of you that accepted everything as it was just like you had all these years. As far as both of these parts of you knew, there was only one man that had right over you and that was Paaji. No one else would ever be allowed access to your body. It was as if Paaji had strapped a chastity belt around your waist and your heart that was invisible to the outside world.

All the things he had said and done to you since you were 11 left you without your own identity. Every day since you were a little girl, his touch, gaze, words, and rewards of praise had secretly ripped off pieces of yourself and replaced them bit by bit like paper maché—strip by strip of pieces conditioned by him until he became your identity. Like a slave, here you now stood where you had no self and identity without him, your master. You didn't know how to live without him. You didn't know how to survive. He was your shadow, your master, your lifeline.

You couldn't make sense of it all. Usually he ignored his wife and didn't seem loving toward her. To you, he said he didn't love her. He gave you extra attention. He would look across the room at you with the familiar glazed eyes you had seen before. He would stay up late long after everyone else had gone to bed. He told you how beautiful you were and how he couldn't live without you. He would cup your face in his hands, smooth your hair, and rub your neck. He would have your body when he pleased.

As it tends to do, life went on in its usual peculiar confusing way. A year later, you were accepted into Simon Fraser University. You moved back to Vancouver to pursue your studies, now away from Paaji.

With Love,

Jeeti

PART THREE

Courageous

LETTER 10

You Are Not Alone

Dear Salakshana,

I was two years into my studies during the Spring semester of 1990 at Simon Fraser University when I suddenly had to take time off.

Nothing I studied would sink into my brain. My brain felt like mush and refused to absorb information from my courses. It was as if it had taken off, leaving behind an empty head. I was super stressed, and it felt as if my brain was cracking. There was always an uneasiness inside me, a feeling of not belonging that came from me not knowing how to live in the world without Paaji.

I felt I didn't belong in Vancouver. It felt as if I didn't belong anywhere except with Paaji. I felt loved, safe, and secure with some sort of sense of belonging in the world that Paaji created for me. Living in a different city, in a world out there without him, did not feel right. It felt awkward, uncomfortable, unfitting, lonely, and unsafe. A part of me always felt uneasy and never at rest. I did not feel normal in a world everyone else called normal. I was 21 years old, lost and confused. In many ways, it felt peculiar. The previous world that I knew before Paaji entered my life was no longer a safe world for me. I felt the new world created by Paaji over the past decade was my normal world now. To leave it felt like a death sentence, like being thrown out into the Sahara desert without a drop of water or shade from the torturous sun.

So, I decided I was going to enter the workforce. I had a brilliant idea. Instead of working for someone else, I thought it would be wise to open a family business. My love for fabrics, my passion to design and create my own ensembles, and my entrepreneurial mind fixated on opening a fabric shop. I looked into opening a fabric shop in Vancouver and realized it would require too much capital. Leasing costs and the amount of inventory required were way too much.

"How about Edmonton?" I asked my Uncle in Williams Lake. In my mind this would also allow me a reason to move back to Edmonton and be close to Paaji.

My family in Williams Lake, Uncle, Massi, and Mom were all for it. Dad? Not so much. He wanted me to finish university and get married. Good thing for me, your marriage, Salakshana, did not work out. Otherwise, Dad would have married me off right after high school as he had done with you. Our parents thought having our family in Edmonton would be great support. Plus, you were there as an extra hand when I would need help.

That summer I moved to Edmonton to live with you and my niece, Chandani, to run our new family business. You were a single, divorced mom now that your husband had left, and you were still living with our Edmonton family. It was around this time Paaji's wife left him. She had suspected something between Paaji and me, and so had his parents. So, the couple divorced.

Embarking on a new venture where I would be surrounded by exquisite silk fabrics was exciting. The Paaji factor had a lot to do with it as well. By now I had stopped calling him Paaji and started referring to him by his name, Manjit. It felt odd to call him Paaji, or brother, when I was now 21 years old. The word would not roll off my tongue as easily as it once did. It felt uncomfortable. I would say his real name in a lower voice, all the while scared and looking around to see if I would get in trouble for calling him by his name. I didn't. Paaji was now Manjit to me.

Soon after the fabulous July opening of our new fabric business, a call from Kira shook my core. It was late evening, and I had just come home from work. Kira told me that you, Salakshana, had learned that Manjit had touched the private parts of another young one, The Little One. This had happened a couple of years ago when The Little One was around 10 years old. Now, The Little One was 12 and had confided in you, Salakshana.

Frightened and distraught, I told The Little One, who was in the house when I received the call, that we would confront Manjit. I asked our Massi who had come from Williams Lake at the time to help out with the business to come with me and confront Manjit. My legs felt like bricks as I mounted the stairs from the basement suite toward the upstairs living room on that warm summer day. I was scared. My insides were racing. My heart was pounding. I was shrinking internally, but on the outside, I pretended to be confident. I had to look confident as The Little One was following right behind me. I couldn't show my fears. I couldn't show I was scared inside about confronting him and revealing the truth. I had to be strong and unafraid of what Manjit would say.

I approached the top of the staircase. The house seemed awkwardly dark except for the dim light coming from the living room. Everyone else in the house had gone to sleep. There was so much weight resting on my shoulders. A part of me wished what had been revealed wasn't true. That it was a misunderstanding and Manjit would have some sort of an explanation to explain the truth. The wiser part of me believed The Little One was telling the truth. I clung to that wiser part. I was going to stand up for The Little One no matter what.

In the living room, the TV was on. Massi sat on the sofa chair and didn't say much. Manjit was lying on the plush sofa with his head hanging low, almost as if he knew what I was going to ask him. Just like that, I told him what The Little One had told us.

He denied it, claiming it was an accidental touch while they had been wrestling. The Little One fired back with the truth, standing strong as tears rolled down the beautiful innocent face. My heart broke for The Little One, whom I loved so dearly.

"I can't believe you would think this way about me," he said in reply.

He defended himself over and over again with his head hung so low, almost as if he was the one so deeply wounded. He acted as if we were bestowing evilness upon him.

"Feel sympathy for me. Poor me," his body language hollered. I was in deep turmoil. A part of me wanted to yell at him at the top of my lungs to just tell the truth. A part of me wanted to punch and slap him as he sat and played victim.

The conversation, if I can even call it that, lasted about 20 minutes with long moments of silence where he wouldn't answer or say anything back. Confronting him didn't result in anything, and I didn't know what else to do. I was scared—scared from this truth, scared from what had happened to The Little One, and scared of what my parents would do to me if they found out I confronted Manjit.

My soul shook at the thought of Mom finding out. I knew for a fact if Mom and Dad got wind of Manjit inappropriately touching The Little One or anyone else in our extended or immediate family, my life would be on the line. It would be my head that would be chopped off. I knew without a doubt I would be the one punished. I would be sent away and married off. I knew all the adults around me would make it all about how rotten and disgraced I was without giving any attention to the truth that was just revealed. They would have made it all about me. The Little One would have been cared for and looked after, but I, on the other hand, would have been shamed, blamed, and abandoned. I wanted my family to love me. I wanted to keep my loved ones in my life. I didn't want to be disowned and abandoned forever. I told my Massi I wasn't going to tell Mom. And that night, I went to bed numb to myself, wounded, disoriented, and shattered.

Salakshana, what can I say? When it rains it pours. Two months after learning about The Little One, Kira gave me some more gut-wrenching news. This time she told me in person.

Kira was visiting from Vancouver for my birthday. We were sitting on the mattress watching TV in the downstairs living room. It was autumn, a very cold and dark late November evening. I had come home from work. You, Salakshana, had been very emotional, and Kira had consoled you earlier that evening. You and Chandani were now sleeping. The night felt later than it was.

"I have to tell you something," said Kira.

"What?" I asked, oblivious to the sledgehammer that stood above my head. I could sense her uncomfortableness. She was sitting close to me. We usually sat close to each other. Many times over the years, she would lie beside me, place her head on my chest, and hug me with her arms as we lay and watched TV. I would run my hand through her hair.

I loved my sister.

"Manjit has done stuff to Salakshana," she said. "That's why she is so messed up and upset and angry all the time. That's why she is always crying and emotional. She told me this evening, and she was hysterical and distraught."

Kira was looking at me straight in the face as she spoke. Her eyes shared so much with me in that moment, telling a grim tale. I stared at her as I absorbed the news. Kira was a loyal sister who I loved and trusted without question.

"He has done it to me, too," she added.

I stayed silent, frozen, sitting up straight as tears quietly rolled down my eyes. On its own, my head lowered, breaking our gaze as my brain tried to comprehend her words.

"I'm so sorry," she said. "I know how fond you are of him, and I don't want to hurt you."

The next day, when Manjit came home from work in the evening, I confronted him. I was distraught, but I wasn't hysterical. I kept a calm demeanour as I shared what Kira had said and asked him if it was all true.

"I did not do anything with Kira," he denied. "But I did with Salakshana. It was only once. I am sorry. It is you that I love."

I sat quietly, motionless as he answered. Inside, I felt the tsunami hit as a tear rolled down my cheek. The feeling that something inside me had died consumed my body once again. This time it was different.

This time, the vibrant Jeeti had died.

My world as I knew it collapsed under the weight and darkness of what Manjit had done. I was too young to be equipped to handle the horror of the news I had received, one after another. It was 10 years ago, October 1980, when Manjit had made me his for the first time. How could I ever forget that dark autumn and its significance in shaping me? For a decade, life had been crazy and incomprehensible. It took immense effort, strength, and courage every day to add joy, beauty, and colour into my life simply to survive. After learning about you, Kira, and The Little One, I faced my darkest day of all.

Alone. Scared. Lifeless. In my now colourless world.

Gone were the dazzling vivid images of the songs from the Bollywood movies. Gone was the magical high of life from the Bollywood tunes that played in my mind during the day, in my sleep, and in my dreams. Gone were the colours of Holi, the festival of colour I had seen in numerous Bollywood movies. Gone were all the colours that had allowed me to survive in Manjit's dark, pitch black world. He had stripped each and every colour from my life. Gone was my heart and any sound of a heart beat.

Gone was Jeeti.

I had so many questions. How could I have loved him so much? How could I have been so blind? How could I have believed him all these years and let him make a fool out of me? How did I fail to see what he was doing? How could I have been so stupid? I felt so much shame, guilt, and emptiness inside.

A conversation with Rani, our Vancouver cousin, from when I was 16 years old, drifted into my mind.

"Hey Jeeti, come here," she had said as she climbed down the attic bedroom ladder of her house. "I have to talk to you girls. Manjit is a snake, so make sure you girls stay away from him. You got that?

I nodded, not knowing what she was talking about. Had he done something to her, too? Of course he had. Why had I been so naive? So dumb? How could I let him do this to my sisters? Why did I believe all his lies? What was wrong with me? All I saw was pitch black all around me. I felt defeated, worthless, so unloved, and extremely separate from everyone, including my sisters, family, and my own self. I felt used, betrayed, smothered, lifeless, completely empty, and in disbelief at the lie I had been living for the past ten years.

I was broken.
Completely shattered.
Destroyed.
Annihilated.
Never to be put back together again.

I didn't drink bleach, contemplate taking rat poison, or mix "do not eat" packages into rice pudding as you had, Salakshana. I didn't think of looking for bullets to load Dad's gun like Kira had. I didn't go looking for train tracks, a river to jump into, a bridge to jump off of, or a knife to slit my wrists as I had seen women do in countless Bollywood movies. I didn't call Kira, whom I loved so dearly and had shared so many of my secrets with. I could not involve her. I could not do that to her. I loved her too much to give her my pain.

Alone, I walked into the washroom, opened the medicine cabinet, and took out a bottle of Kira's pills she had accidentally left behind from her recent visit. I remembered when Kira took one of these pills she would sleep the entire day.

If I take all of them, I thought, *I will sleep forever.*

I had no idea how to deal with the unbearable pain of betrayal or how to remove the sharp dagger that had ripped open my heart. It was now a wounded heart which, with each throb, pumped intense pain through my being. I felt I was in the darkest unknown swamplands, all alone with no one to talk to and no way out. I did not want to live this way anymore. I did not want to be part of this life anymore—a life that had left me and betrayed me so horribly. I'd had enough. All those times I wished I was dead, and now, that time had finally arrived.

I was completely alone with nowhere to go and nowhere to hide.

I stood staring at myself in the washroom mirror, disassociated from what I saw. I stared back at the numb, lifeless Jeeti, not recognizing who she was anymore. The tears that rolled down my cheeks could not wash away my sorrows. They couldn't come fast enough to heal my wounds and liberate me from the dungeon of grief, sadness, and despair. They could not cleanse my soul that was being shadowed by evil. I emptied the bottle of Kira's pills into the palm of my hand. I looked at the cluster of tiny pills. There must have been around 30 of them. All at once, I tossed them into my mouth and drank the water from my glass.

Immediately, I knew I had done something so completely wrong. I tried to put my finger down my throat but couldn't shove it deep enough to vomit. I failed miserably at trying to shove my toothbrush down my throat. A few seconds after taking the pills, a tingly feeling came over my head. The pills were starting to take effect, pulling me into the quicksand of darkness. I took one last look at myself in the mirror and went into my bed, a mattress in the living room of the basement suite. I crawled under my comforter and pulled it up to my face underneath my chin.

"I love you, Kira. I love you, Mom. I am so sorry."

I whispered into the lonely air. I felt a tear roll down my

cheek. My eyes automatically started closing. I did not resist closing them, welcoming a deep eternal sleep forever.

I was out cold for two and a half days. Salakshana, you tried talking to me while I was out cold. You thought I was sick. Our Masser from upstairs came downstairs the second day and asked me what was wrong with me.

"If you are sick, go see a doctor," he said.

I couldn't open my eyes; I couldn't answer him. I was like a corpse. My family thought I was sick, but Manjit knew otherwise. Still, he did nothing to help me. I could feel his presence as I came in and out of consciousness for a second or two. I knew he was sitting there quietly watching TV. No one got me help. The family around me, including Manjit, carried on with life without me.

On the third day, I woke up groggy, with nothing making sense to me. Finally, I got up. I managed to go to work at the fabric store. It had remained closed, out cold just like me. I was the only one who opened it. It was the first week of December, and Christmas was right around the corner. It was the first Christmas I didn't go back home to Williams Lake.

For a good couple of weeks, I felt like I was in the twilight zone with the effects of the pills weighing heavily on my brain and body. The long-term effects lasted months, perhaps even years. I lived life in a daze.

I had failed miserably at taking my own life.

What a disgrace I was.

With Love,

Jeeti

LETTER 11

Believe In Miracles

Dear Young Jeeti,

As you lay in deep, dark sleep, unconscious and thinking you were dead, the word "miracle" somehow inscribed itself into your life with all its essence.

Miracle: a surprising and welcome event that is not explicable by natural or scientific laws and is therefore considered to be the work of a divine agency.

That's the dictionary definition.

It was really by some miracle you woke up. You were so out of it, feeling extremely groggy, disassociated from yourself, and giving no thought to what you had done. Your brain did not turn on to remind you of what you had attempted. It made no attempt to tell you what you had done is referred to as suicide. You made zero effort to make sense of what had just transpired. You were numb.

I have to go to work and open the store.

That is the only thought you had. You got up to get ready. You felt a pang of guilt for missing what you thought was only a day of work. The pills were still in effect, making your brain cloudy and spaced out. Everything moved like it was in slow motion, as if all the sound in the world had been turned off. Somehow you did manage to get up, brush your teeth, put on your clothes, drive, and go to work to manage the fabric store you were responsible for.

Once you woke up after taking the pills, something inside you changed. It was as if a switch had flipped. It was like a pilot light of an old furnace was lit, turning the entire ancient system on and sending you a strong signal to stay away from Manjit. You had literally *woken up* in a different way. You no longer wanted to be around him anymore. You felt uneasy around him and had the desire to get away. You knew you had to get away from him. You wanted to put an end to what Manjit was doing to your mind and body. You wanted to change the life he had created for you since you were 11 years old. You wanted him to leave you alone.

It was as if the cord that had tethered you to him for all these years had finally been severed. Cut while you lay unconscious for days. Cut by a silent power that came from a place within you that you didn't know existed. The path that led from your heart to his was no longer there. It stood completely vanished, erased. Your heart beat as if it had been charged with a power of its own. It no longer relied on Manjit for its source of power. The heavy chain that had been fastened to you was broken. The shackles were gone, setting you free of him. Your mind now was its own mind, and your heart was finally free to beat its own rhythm.

Something had changed indeed.

The Little Jeeti he relentlessly groomed and primed for more than a decade had died and rebirthed into a Jeeti that was ready to claim her worth and power. As horrible and dark as it was for you to walk into the arms of death, you had succeeded beyond your imagination in killing the immaculately groomed Jeeti so she could be reborn into a Jeeti who would groom herself as she pleased. She would bloom in whatever colour she chose. You allowed her to resurrect herself with strength and courage to take the steps to control her own mind, free herself from Manjit's power and confinement, and make better choices. You freed her from a prison deadlier than Alcatraz.

It was without question very painful for you to learn the truth of what he had inflicted on your sisters. You had to overcome the confusion in your mind from the years of conditioning and grooming by this man. It was mentally cumbersome for you to hack away at the web Manjit had spun with great precision all around you. You had to uninstall each and every state of the art software program he had downloaded into you. Learning he had crossed all sexual boundaries with your sisters and realizing he had used you as his sex slave helped you to break away from his robust web. As painful as it was to learn the truth and face one dark moment after another, it strengthened you and freed you beyond your limits.

You now knew Manjit was a deadly, toxic poison you had to get away from. He had to be banished from your life. You awoke as a much more determined Jeeti that would stand up for herself and use her voice to fight back against Manjit. You knew he would never let it be easy. You knew separating yourself from him was something that wouldn't happen all in one day. The process of separating yourself from him started bit by bit, day by day. You chipped away at it slowly, doing your best under the circumstances.

Jeeti, you were a miracle. All your guides and angels—a greater force—had been watching over you. The Universe blessed you with another chance at life. There were other miracles eagerly waiting to come your way. Day by day you started restructuring and stepped onto the path of developing your own true self, figuring out who *you* were, what *you* wanted, and where *you* wanted to be in life.

Not around Manjit.

It was the opposite of what you had felt before. Now you felt he would swallow you into darkness if you did not escape him. He would pull you by your ankles back into the quicksand of despair. You knew he was dangerous. You knew he had no place in your life. You were a free bird, and now your entire being longed to run away from Manjit and the prison he had created for you.

It wasn't that easy for you, was it? You had just started the family business and were bound by a three-year lease and your commitment to run the store. You lived with your sister and your Edmonton family in the same house as him, and changing living arrangements was not something that would happen immediately. You had to be patient and keep calm. You had to ensure Manjit wouldn't sniff your thoughts and come to know you had changed. He couldn't know of your plan to set yourself free.

No matter what, you wanted out.

With Love,

Jeeti

LETTER 12

Love Will Find You

Dear Young Jeeti,

Oh, Jeeti.

Sweet, 22-year-old Jeeti.

You were very blessed to have failed at taking your own life. Not in your wildest dreams could you have imagined that a handsome young man would come riding into your life. You believed your childhood dreams of having a husband and a family had been crushed by Manjit, locked up in a chest and thrown away forever. You had convinced yourself fairytales only came true for girls who were "pure." Without a doubt, you knew your culture would never accept a dishonoured girl like you. You had no hopes of ever getting married. You believed you were disgraced, and no man would ever want you.

Never could you have allowed yourself to imagine what happened next.

The most handsome young man with large eyes in shades of green, hazel, and light brown unexpectedly came into your life. A man full of so much love, life, and brightness. A man whose ear-to-ear smile was so bright it took your breath away and made your heart flutter. A man your heart was compelled to call *Sohna, (mean-*

ing beautiful, attractive, handsome, precious, beloved in Punjabi).

You met Sohna almost two months after you had tried to take your own life. You were not looking for a man or a relationship. You had never had a boyfriend. You always ran away from boys who showed any interest other than friendship. You had many male friends through high school and university, but that's all they ever were—only friends. You were not looking for love.

Jeeti, my dear, *love found you.*

You and Sohna first saw each other as young adults at his nephew's Lohri party. Lohri is an Indian occasion in mid-January celebrating the birth of a son or the wedding of a son. Even though your families had known each other, you and Sohna did not. He was wearing an olive green silk charmeuse shirt with matching pants that night. You were wearing a hot pink and purple Bollywood inspired silk dress that came to your knees in the front and reached your ankles in the back. It was a one-of-a-kind piece you had made yourself out of embroidered crêpe de chine silk. The bodice was fitted to the waist, coming down in the front in a v-shape toward your navel. The dress was pleated at the waist and flared at the bottom. The front of the dress came to the knees while the back came almost to your ankles, supported by a tight raw silk pajami and a chunni. He had a well-kept mustache and long dark hair that flowed as he danced with grace. You were a blonde with the 80's bangs and long curly hair permed to perfection. He was tall and slender. You had the perfect curves.

Initially, you didn't pay much attention to him. But at the end of the night, your car wouldn't start. The carburetor had flooded, something it did every now and then. You knew how to fix it by opening the hood and letting the excessive fuel evaporate. All you needed was a screwdriver. Salakshana went back inside to ask for one. A few minutes later, there was a tap on your driver side window. It was Sohna. His sister had sent him in place of a screwdriver to help start up your car. He was crouched by your window, smiling ear to ear. You rolled down the window and smiled back.

"My car engine floods," you told him, "and I usually pop up the hood and use a screwdriver to start it."

"Turn on the ignition and press on the gas pedal as hard as you can," he said.

"It's not working," you told him as you did.

"Harder," he said. "Keep pressing the pedal as far as you can."

"I am," you replied as you pressed down hard.

The engine started to make a noise as it tried to start.

"More," he said.

You pressed down as hard as you could.

"More," he repeated.

To your surprise the car started. You laughed and thanked him.

"He's so cute," you said to Salakshana as you drove off. You thought about his large warm eyes and bright smile on the drive home. It made you smile.

It was a month later you asked Salakshana to call him. You had wanted to go to an Indian dance. It was a family dance, and these kinds of dances in the Indian community were uncommon back then. You, Jeeti, felt you needed a male chaperone and didn't want to go without one. You didn't have any male friends in Edmonton and didn't know who to ask. For some reason, Sohna came to mind. So, you asked Salakshana to call him. She was classified as a married woman, had lived in Edmonton longer than you, and had interacted with his family as well as spoken to him a few times over the years when he had come over to Masser's house. His family was traditional, and it was not accepted in the community for Indian girls to call males. Still, Salakshana dialed the number. She was a little nervous, but luckily it was Sohna who answered.

He accompanied you girls to the dance. It was a fun night. You all chatted in the car until 4:30 a.m. despite the snow and cool February temperature. Thereafter, he started to pay quick visits to your work. His energy was as succulent, soft, and sumptuous as the silks in your store. Something inside you lit up when he dropped by. You felt tingles at his slightest touch, and his hugs were full of warmth. The green in his eyes sparkled like a peridot with so much joy and life. Unexpectedly, he leaned in and kissed you on your neck one day. You didn't like that. You froze. It brought up a fear inside you. You turned your face away.

He's like the rest of the males, you thought. *How could he do this? How could he think I was that kind of a girl?*

This is not what you wanted, so you decided to have a talk with him the next day to let him know that. You didn't want him to kiss you. You didn't want him to do that ever again.

"We are just friends," you said, making the boundaries clear.

"Yes," he agreed sincerely with his warm eyes and smile.

Oh, innocent Jeeti, the boundaries were soon washed away by his daily bright presence in your life and the safety and openness you felt with him. The boundaries had crumbled under the joy he exuded and infected you with. You didn't know what was happening to you. The tingling sensations that overtook your body made your heart beat like a Dhol *(an Indian drum used in Bhangra, Punjabi folk dance)*. The very thought of him ignited explosions of sensations and feelings through your being. A long lost symphony started playing in your soul. You fell into the safety of his arms. You, my dear, had fallen in love with him. You connected soul to soul and could feel your souls dancing in the flames of love. You couldn't believe it. You couldn't comprehend how suddenly and unexpectedly your hearts were being woven together by the sutra of love. There was this unexplainable magnetic pull between you two. You did not try and make sense of it all with your mind. You followed your heart and listened to the silent whispers from your soul that guided you to him.

He coloured your world and showed you what love was. You went with him on dates where you explored the finest foods and sampled the best of wines. You had never experienced a date before. He bought you your very first flowers, chocolates, and more. He showed you true love, and you happily gave love back to him. He brought so much joy and excitement into your life. You laughed, you danced, and once again, you felt like a Bollywood princess. It was so surreal. It was so magical, like a fairytale playing out in real life. It was true love. It was how a man is supposed to love a woman.

You were alive. The vibrant, vivacious Jeeti was back and ready to write more new chapters in her life. That year you, Salakshana, and your niece Chandani moved out of Massi, Masser, and Manjit's house. You were so hopeful for a fresh start.

When Sohna came into your life, it was as if the Universe knew to send him your way. Manjit did not like the fact you were out spending time with Sohna. He tried desperately to keep you in his grip. He took on all the characteristics of a violent, angry, and jealous man—the kind you had seen as a villain in the Bollywood movies. He followed you around. He would ask Salakshana and Chandani, a little child herself, about your whereabouts. You would see his car through your rear view mirror following you. You were scared of what he might do to Sohna and of what he might do to humiliate you in front of Sohna.

He was stalking you. You would confront him. He would be upset and act as if he wasn't doing all the horrible things. Still, he would show up at Salakshana's house and wait for you until you came home in the evenings. He wouldn't leave you alone. He wanted to touch you. You did not want to be touched by him. In fact, you even had a moment when you wanted to kill him once in late November 1992 when he tried to force himself on you. It was late evening while you were in bed. You fought him off hard as he mounted you. You called out Sohna's name for help as you tried super hard to close your legs.

"I like it when you call me Sohna," he said.

Your mind raced to find what you could hit him with. You saw a Bollywood VHS video laying on the floor out of your reach and imagined hitting him on the head. Then you saw the scissors in the corner lying beside the Christmas wrapping paper. They too were far away from your reach. You imagined stabbing him with the scissors. You thought about stabbing him hard in the back as he was wrestling with you. You wanted to save yourself and your body. All of a sudden, he stopped forcing himself on you; he had ejaculated. Your struggle had excited him. You had somehow managed to save yourself from being raped that night.

The stalking continued, and Manjit became more violent. He scared the hell out of you when he punched out Sohna's car window late at night. You and Sohna were in the car savouring sweet long kisses. You both didn't notice a vehicle with its headlights turned off approaching you in the dark. You screamed in horror when you heard a loud bang and saw Manjit's fist had shattered glass all over Sohna and the car seat.

"Fuck, it's Manjit," said Sohna.

Manjit was yelling for you to get out of the car. Sohna got out of the car. By the time you got out, he had punched Sohna in the face. Sohna was bleeding; Manjit had punched him on the nose. Sohna put his hands to his injured face while Manjit rushed to hold him in a headlock.

"Let him go," you screamed repeatedly as you pushed at Manjit. You could smell alcohol off of him. He had a mad look on his face, his eyes red with rage, furrowed eyebrows and nostrils flaring. You knew he had gone crazy. You knew he would harm Sohna further. He would have no mercy on your lover.

"I am going to tell him everything," yelled Manjit. "Come home with me, or I am going to tell him everything. Come home with me. Come home with me right now."

"Okay, okay," you said, scared, confused, powerless, and afraid for Sohna's life.

Manjit let go of Sohna. You complied and followed Manjit to his car, crying. You realized it was your car that he was driving. He had brought it from your house when he noticed Kira had come home without you. He had come looking for you in the night. You looked at Sohna as you got into the car and saw him fixing himself up. You were so distraught and traumatized that you didn't even say goodbye to Sohna. Your heart broke. You didn't even get the chance to ask him if he was okay. You knew if you didn't leave with Manjit, Sohna's life was in grave danger.

Manjit would kill him.

It was a quick, two minute car ride home. Manjit was saying stuff about how much he loved you and was watching out for you. He talked about how Sohna was using you and would never marry you. You were in disbelief, angry, distraught, and zoned out. You sat quietly afraid beside him. He took you straight home to where you lived in Salakshana's house. You went inside and told Kira what he had done. Thank goodness Kira was there to help you with the family business. Kira stood face to face with him, told him off, and asked him to leave.

"I'm going to tell everyone what you did to me," she yelled as she pointed her finger at him.

"You hooker!" he yelled back to her.

He shoved her with both hands, pushing her a step back. You were certain he was going to hit Kira. You got in the middle of them to protect her. He attempted to push Kira from over top of you. You put your hands on his chest trying to hold him back, asking him not to do this. He finally backed off and left.

A day later, you found out he had called Mom that night to tell her about your rendezvous with Sohna. He had also called Sohna's house to speak with Sohna's older brother. Manjit told you all of this. He was boasting about it himself. He had always threatened you that he would tell. Still, the danger for Sohna grew as Manjit continued with his threats.

"There are people here to kill him. People from Vancouver," he told you with his evil grin at the Diwali function later that year. Sohna was there performing Bhangra with his dance team.

"They are going to kill him. They are going to kill him with a knife. They even have a gun," Manjit taunted you.

"Why would someone want to kill him? Did you hire them?" you asked.

"I don't know. You will see. They are here to kill him, and they are going to kill him tonight," he repeated with delight. You wanted to wipe the huge evil grin off his face. "He is going to die today."

You pretended to ignore him and hide your fear, consoling yourself and doing your best to believe that what he was saying wouldn't be so and that his ramblings were nothing but empty threats. Instead of a celebration of the light over darkness, Diwali became something else for you: a worry for your lover's life. Somehow someone in Sohna's circle of friends caught wind of Manjit's plan and told Sohna to leave out of a back door. Manjit then smirked, flashing his teeth, and accused Sohna of being a coward. You were disgusted with Manjit's vile remarks. You turned around and walked away feeling helpless, sad, and with a heart full of sorrow knowing that your beloved was in grave danger. Your eyes glimpsed over every corner of the party hall to take one look at Sohna to make sure he was okay. You could not see him. You searched the entire place and could not locate him. In your heart, you knew he was gone. You knew he was safe.

The stalking, physical violence, and death threats from Manjit could not keep Sohna and you apart. You both loved each other, and your love grew stronger with each passing day. You lived in fear for your beloved's life, but you did not cave into Manjit's threats of killing Sohna or his threats of exposing you to Sohna and his family for what a dirty girl you really were. Sohna didn't think much else of Manjit's actions except that Manjit was being an angry "brother" who was trying to protect his sister and her family honour. In Indian culture back then (and in many places still today), girls are not supposed to date. It was common for brothers, cousins, uncles, and fathers to go after and beat up males that dated their girls.

As you were battling Manjit, Sohna had a battle of his own brewing in his family. Sohna was the youngest of seven living children, two older sisters followed by two older brothers and then two more older sisters. There was a vast age difference between his eldest siblings and him. His older sisters were your Mom's age, and he was closer in age to you, only two years older. You were now 24, and he was 26. His family was thinking it was time for him to settle and marry. His older brother and old aunt (his Phua) held the power in the family and were the head family figures. They were three brothers living together as a joint family. His two older brothers were married, and his older brother was the eldest male in the household with children, so he was the father figure.

"It's time for us to find you a girl," said his older brother one weekend.

"I have already found one," said Sohna.

"Who?" he asked, fully knowing that Sohna and I were seeing each other.

"Jeeti," answered Sohna.

Sohna's brother and his Phua became very upset once he mentioned your name. It all blew up from there. Sohna's family was a very traditional Indian family. His family held on to old traditional values while your parents were more moderate and had assimilated in many ways into Canadian culture. They did not approve of him marrying you. They did not see you in a good light. Certainly, conversations between Sohna's older brother and Salakshana's divorced husband years back did not paint a good picture of you. Your physical appearance didn't help. You were the opposite of what they were looking for in a suitable match for their household: westernized, outgoing, independent, running a business. You had blond hair, wore makeup and shorts, and had many male friends. They wanted to arrange his wedding to a traditional Punjabi Sikh subservient girl that would fit their traditional Punjabi family and keep their familial financial structure together. A girl that was "pure" and not so influenced by Canadian culture. A girl they could control as they controlled him.

You were not that girl.

They wanted to keep traditional law and order in their household. Sohna knew all along his family would oppose his desire to marry you. It tore him apart. For Sohna, it would be either them or you. His older brother and his Phua drew the line.

You loved Sohna beyond what words could ever express, and there was no doubt in your mind of how much he loved you. His every look, touch, and kiss sent electric pulses through you. It was as if you had travelled together for centuries as sweethearts, as souls, as an eternal flame. Every day the drumming of his heartbeat echoed his love for you. *Boom, Boom, Boom.* You would hear it every time you laid your head against his chest. Your heart matched his drumming, filled with intense love—a love that came from an ancient sacred place and conveyed your true value.

Sohna enabled you to open the gateway that allowed you to feel that you did have value. He helped you see that you were valued and worthy of love. He saw much deeper value in you than strictly your body and its pureness. Not once did he question your honour. He did not check the white bed sheets for your virgin blood.

Contrary to what you were led to believe by your culture and upbringing, it takes a man of great value to overlook that detail.

With Love,

Jeeti

LETTER 13

You Will Be Silenced

Dear Young Jeeti,

You went back home to Williams Lake for Christmas in 1992 to spend the holiday with your parents, siblings, extended family and friends. It was the same house you had moved into in 1974. You and your sister Kira were in the washroom where nothing much had changed. It stood adorned in its 1970's glory and bore witness to you children growing up. It kept to itself the many secret conversations over the decades between you sisters, your three Massis, and Mom. It was the only place in the house where you females felt you had privacy. You felt a closeness and intimacy in this space. That's why it was the chosen space for an important conversation that was about to take place.

Kira and The Little One wanted to tell Mom about Manjit touching them inappropriately.

"Go ahead," you said.

You were going to support your sister Kira and The Little One no matter what. This time you did not dwell on what would happen to you. From the knot in your stomach, your 24-year-old self knew exactly how the conversation was going to go, but you wanted it to happen either way.

Kira called Mom and your Massi into the washroom. She and The Little One told Mom about Manjit. Mom turned on the faucet so no one outside the washroom would be able to hear the conversation.

"Chup karo kuti-o. Tere pai nei sun laina," she whispered, meaning, *"Be quiet bitches, your father will hear you."*

She immediately ignored Kira and The Little One and turned her body toward you. You were sitting silent on the edge of the bathtub.

"Tera Sohna nal viah nahi hona," she said looking down at me, meaning, *"You will never be able to marry Sohna."*

"Tu apna soch la," she said pointing her hand full out toward me, meaning, *"Think about yourself!"*

With that said, she marched out of the washroom, giving no care to her daughters or The Little One she had just hurt. Massi followed Mom out, covering her ears and saying, "I can't listen to this."

Even though you knew this was exactly how the conversation would go—with fingers pointed at you—you were still stunned hearing it aloud from your own mother. You hadn't even opened your mouth to say anything. Instead of listening to Kira and The Little One, Mom targeted you. She knew by doing so Kira and The Little One would shut up. Kira would never blow up your life and get you in trouble. Kira and The Little One were left shocked. You were silenced by a woman you adored, cherished, and looked up to. A woman you thought was God. A woman who did not ask if you were okay. A woman who didn't want any other details of your lifelong ordeal. You stared at the floor, wrapped in the arms of shame instead of the arms of a nurturing mother. With her few words, Mom had just cut off your tongue.

You looked up at Kira. She was angry. The Little One looked helpless. You were scared, disappointed (at Mom and yourself), and knew there was nothing more you could do to help Kira and The Little One. Your eyes locked with Kira's, sensing each other's powerlessness and confusion over what to do. Mom had smothered her own daughters and The Little One in the blanket of shame with her bare hands.

Months later, Spring of 1993, you were totally caught off guard when Sohna unexpectedly told you that Manjit had called him four months back to share something very disturbing. It was evident to you Sohna was uncomfortable and struggling to find the right words. He expressed how stupid it felt to even bring it up and ask.

"What is it?" you asked, looking into his eyes as fear crawled up your body inch by inch. In your core, you knew what he was about to ask.

He stated Manjit had shared that the two of you had a thing. It was something that would never end, and it would continue even once you married. Instantly, you froze. Everything around you came to a sudden halt. Time stood still. This was the moment you had always dreaded. The most dreadful moment that would snatch you from your newfound life and happiness and throw you back into the darkness you had closed the door on. This was the instant it would all be taken away. You felt death looming on top of you once again. Your mind raced trying to figure out what to do.

Suddenly, Mom came up in your mind.

How would she have me respond to this? you thought. *How would she have me swear on her life? With the truth or a lie?*

You knew the answer. It came up instantly. You didn't need much time to think it through. You knew what you had to do. You looked at Sohna and told him it wasn't true, swearing on your mother's life. The lump in your throat had grown so large, it was threatening to constrict your airways as you held yourself together inside. You had just lied to your beloved, the love of your life, adding more weight to the tapestry of shame and guilt being woven daily into your life. All you wanted was to be loved and to give love. You felt like a disgrace, committing the ultimate sin of all: betrayal.

Manjit had used the hidden secret as blackmail and had threatened to tell Sohna numerous times. You just didn't know when he would do it. You also knew he would do everything in his power to destroy you and Sohna. You never knew what he would do next.

Jeeti, it took a lot of bravery and courage on your part to stand up to Manjit over and over again. It was indeed very difficult for you to attempt to reclaim what was yours: your voice, your power, and your right to a good life. You drew from the power of love you and Sohna shared to not cave under the fear of Manjit. Although you were very scared, you chose to face whatever came next. The more you dug into your inner power and stood for what you wanted and what was right for you, the more his remaining bits of power over you dwindled. You became more courageous and vocal. Each and every confrontation of the past and present built layers of strength in you—a strength that helped you regain your personal power, voice, and identity. When he snarled like a beast, you stood straight and looked him in the eye. You had tapped into the bold, vibrant, and vivacious Jeeti you once were.

Of course it wasn't easy to free yourself from Manjit. It didn't happen overnight. He would show up whenever he pleased. You had to be polite, make compromises, and pick your battles with him so he wouldn't hurt Sohna. What had become easy now was to disconnect from the power he held over you. Now, you could see life for what it really was. You could clearly see what you wanted and what you didn't want. You didn't want anything to do with Manjit and the past you had lived. You desired Sohna and wanted to build a life full of love and joy with him. You wanted a happy life with Sohna, a house with a white picket fence, and a family of your own. You wanted to be allowed to be you, the Jeeti you were born to be.

In 1993, once the lease for your business expired, you moved from Edmonton back to Vancouver to finish your last year of University at SFU and obtain your degree. You knew you had to move far away from Manjit and his threats to bring your life on track. It was soon after you moved that it became evident that Mom wanted whatever Manjit had done to be kept quiet forever. She pretended as if it never happened and as if she never knew. Manjit was divorced, and Mom had thought about marrying him to her niece in India. Despite the age difference (she was 19 and he was 33), she thought it was a good idea so her niece could immigrate to Canada. When you and Kira found out about Mom's plans, you were enraged. Given all that had happened, you did not want Manjit to marry your cousin on your Mom's side of the family. To you, that was so sick and twisted.

You called Mom and questioned her, telling her she could not go through with her plans. Mom was angry. You handed the phone over to Kira, who had more than a mouthful to say to Mom. She threatened to expose Manjit to everyone and more. Finally, Mom backed off her plan.

Moving far away from Manjit was liberating for you. You thought you were finally free.

Still, you carried with you the pain of parting from Sohna when you moved. It was extremely difficult and painful, yet it was the right thing to do. The thought of his family not allowing him to marry you jabbed like a sword in your heart.

How much more would you have to bleed before you could have the wonderful life you so rightfully deserved?

With Love,

Jeeti

LETTER 14

Stand Up For the Truth

Dear Jeeti,

Step by step, slowly placing one foot in front of the other, you at 27 years of age walked down the aisle of the Williams Lake gurdwara, the Guru Nanak Sikh Temple. You saw the back of the groom, your husband to be, sitting on the floor in front of the Guru Granth Sahib *(Sikh holy scriptures)*. He sat tall and slender with perfectly straight posture in his red turban wearing two long strands of pearls on top of a cream silk brocade Achkan *(a knee-length Indian jacket)* and burgundy velvet robe, holding a sword.

The gurdwara was packed with a sea of guests, females sitting on your left side and males sitting on the right. Adorned in the 16 singar *(embellishments)* customary for an Indian bride, including gold jewelry, bright red chura, and an embroidered red silk wedding lehnga with a long train, you walked toward the groom. The long train obeyed your every footstep, following you step by step. Its rustling sent you messages of reassurance of the new life ahead. The loud jingles coming from the ghungroo of your gold anklets echoed that sentiment.

It had been three long years after you left Edmonton. And now, in June 1996, the day had finally come.

This was your wedding day, Jeeti.

You reached the end of the aisle, bowed to the Guru Granth Sahib, and took your place beside the groom. You did not look at him. You kept your head bowed like the good Indian bride you had seen in countless Bollywood movies.

The groom sitting next to you was your beloved Sohna.

He had left his family and his home for you. He was given an ultimatum. He could not return to his family home if he married you. You felt sad for Sohna and cried through the entire ceremony as you were hit with one wave of emotion after another. Your family was very happy for you, and everyone was very excited about your wedding. Some of Sohna's family were present (his mother, two of his sisters with their husbands and family, his second eldest brother with his wife, a niece and her family, and some close friends). In total there were only about 60 people from his side and about 450 from your side.

You left the gurdwara in a horse and carriage. Sohna didn't have anything. He didn't have any belongings, no car, money, or a home to take you to, but that didn't matter to you. All he had was his undying love for you. All he could give you was his heart. That was all you wanted.

It was the start of a new life and the making of a new home. You knew together, you would figure it out. And figure it out you did! You stayed a few months with one of Sohna's sisters and her family, found your own place in a nearby city, borrowed money from your sister Salakshana to start Sohna's business, and a year later, had bought your first house with the financial help of your parents. You soon followed your passion of becoming a fashion designer creating custom made couture. Almost four years later, in the year 2000, you were blessed with the most beautiful baby girl, Maheema.

Like a blink of an eye, the years flew by.

Over the years, Kira mentioned to you how she wanted Mom

and Dad to do something about what Manjit had done to her. She was always getting sick off and on and suffered with what seemed like long bouts of depression. You, Jeeti, always worried about your sister. You loved her so much and knew without ever having to ask that she would always be there for you. She would stand up for you in a heartbeat. You told her to do what she needed to do for herself and not to worry about you. You didn't want her to worry about how coming out with her abuse would affect you and your marriage. You knew it didn't matter which one of your sisters spoke out about Manjit; the fingers would automatically be pointed at you. One peep from your sisters would result in an explosion of shame and blame blown your way by the adults in your family. Still, you didn't want that to be the reason your sisters stayed silent.

It was in 2005, 13 years after the failed washroom conversation with Mom, when Kira attempted once again to tell Mom about what Manjit had done to her. You, Mom, and Kira were sitting in the car outside of Salakshana's brown house in Surrey when Kira brought up the subject. Mom had come to visit you all in Surrey. Summer was in full force, and the sun beamed happily over all of you on this beautiful, bright day. Kira was sitting in the driver's seat, Mom was sitting in the front passenger seat, and you were in the back seat. Mom listened quietly to what Kira had to say, and after Kira was done, you took the bold step of admitting Manjit had done stuff to you, too. You also told her about Papa, her father. You told Mom not to worry about how all this would affect your marriage. You let her know it was okay if Kira wanted to tell everyone about Manjit.

Mom's reaction this time around was different. She said she would talk to Dad, and they would both go talk to Manjit when they went to Edmonton. She didn't display any anger toward you and Kira for bringing up the topic.

But Mom and Dad never did go and talk to Manjit.

Over the years, you would see Manjit from a distance at

various family functions. You always ignored him and pretended you never saw him. You acted as if he wasn't even there. But one particular function made you very uncomfortable.

It was May 2006 at your cousin's engagement party in Edmonton (your Massi and Masser in Edmonton's son). By now, Mom and Dad should have already talked to Manjit about what he had done to Kira. They were supposed to go to his house to do so, but that never happened. At this engagement party, your brother Jesse was hugging and dancing with Manjit. You and Kira felt very uncomfortable. It was sickening for you to see your brother being so jovial and kind to Manjit, not knowing he was embracing a rapist. Kira said she was going to tell Jesse. You thought it was time Jesse should know, so you agreed. Kira pulled Jesse aside and told him a little of what Manjit had done to her. Jesse sat down, upset for the rest of the evening. His distress carried on the next day at the second party. At this party, you noticed Manjit dancing with his second wife and some young girls. One of them was from his sister Parm's side of the family. She must have only been 15; he was 46.

The next day on your way for lunch at Parm's house, Kira showed you a picture. One of the young girls had taken photos on a digital camera. It was a picture of Manjit and the 15-year-old girl. She was holding a drink and Manjit had his arm around her shoulders while his hand rested on top of hers around the glass she held. Looking at the picture made you sick. You felt nauseous. Your stomach turned. You thought instantly Manjit had gotten to this young girl and were concerned. This couldn't be happening. Could he possibly be doing what he did to you and your sisters even today, 25 years later?

Yes.

It hit you like a sledgehammer.

"I'm going to tell Parm," Kira whispered.

Parm was Manjit's youngest sister. She was a close cousin to you, and this young girl in the photo was from her husband's side of the family so it made perfect sense to warn Parm. Kira was seeking your permission, and you gave it without any hesitation. You knew without a doubt it had to be done. Kira had so much love for you and always thought about how her coming out would affect you. You knew the right thing to do was to let Kira do what she needed to do. You did not pay attention to what would happen to you. You would deal with the aftermath as it came.

Kira told Parm that very same day.

"Didn't you say no?" Parm said to Kira when she told her of what Manjit had done.

"I was only a child," stated Kira, perplexed by Parm's comment. Kira went on further to tell Parm she needed to watch over the little girls in her family and household and protect them from her brother. The conversation only lasted a few minutes. Parm made no mention of Kira's conversation to you as she hugged you goodbye that day. She also didn't make any attempt to mention the conversation three months later when she came to visit you in late August at your home in Surrey.

That's why it came as a complete shock to you when on Saturday, September 9, 2006, a phone call came from Parm. You had just finished designing, meticulously creating, and photographing an immaculate shawl collection and were preparing for a big launch.

Parm started the conversation by saying, "Thank you for having us over and your kind hospitality."

You and Sohna had been impeccable hosts, as you always were to family and friends who would come visit. You opened your heart and your home to Parm and her family. You lavished them with a hearty meal and fine wine. Parm and her husband praised you.

"You are just like your dad," they said. "Your dad is a great and very nice man. You are so great, you take after him."

Uncomfortable with all the praise, you brushed off the comments. It was difficult and uncomfortable for you to accept praise. Your love and generosity flowed naturally from your heart; you did not expect any compliments for it.

Then, the phone call shifted. There was no way you could have prepared for what was to come out of her mouth next. She told you one of your sisters had called your Massi that lived in Edmonton, the one who was married to Parm and Manjit's older brother, your Masser. The same Massi and Masser you had lived with in Edmonton when you were younger. Apparently, while Parm and her family were on holiday in Surrey, one of your sisters had called Edmonton and told this Massi that Manjit had sexually abused her as a child. When Parm went back to Edmonton from Surrey, that same Massi told Parm, and Parm decided to call you.

"I didn't know my sister had told that Massi," you said.

"Yeah right! How could you not have known?" Parm questioned you.

You, Jeeti, really had no idea what Parm was talking about. Parm was intent on protecting her brother. You started to get upset when you told Parm of your sisters and cousins who had confided in you that Manjit had sexually abused them or attempted to: Salakshana, Kira, Rani, and Babbu. You mentioned other girls he may have harmed. You also mentioned The Little One. You mentioned Kira was 10, and the Little One was around the same when they were first sexually abused by Manjit. You told her how you were only 11. Parm displayed no compassion or empathy for anyone except her brother.

"How many 10 or 11 year olds want to have sex?" you asked in anger and disbelief.

"There are plenty of 10 year olds that want to have sex," she stated bluntly.

There was no concern on her part of the harm he had done. It was as if he was a saint. She took no notice or consideration of the trauma he had inflicted on you, your sisters, and your cousins.

"My sisters can tell whoever they want and do whatever they feel," you said. "I don't care if he's jailed or if he's hung."

"My poor brother," she said, "My poor brother."

"Poor brother?" you asked. "What about my sisters and all the girls he has done all this horrible stuff to?"

You were shocked and could feel the anger and rage build up inside you.

Ruthlessly, Parm carried on.

"Sare muzay lai ke hun tu rondi ha," she said, meaning, *"After having so much pleasure, now you are crying."*

"Believe me there was not any pleasure with what he did to me," you fired back with your stomach churning in disgust and anger.

You were so angry and upset at Parm. You were enraged. How could she have it so wrong? So twisted? That is not the way it was. That is not the truth. You realized she didn't get it and didn't care to get it. All Parm cared about was protecting her "poor" brother.

"Why are you calling me?" you asked. "I'm not the one who told anyone anything. If it's my sister who told that Massi, then go call her. Why are you calling me?"

"I'm calling you because you can talk to your sisters and keep them quiet. You should think about your marriage. If you want to save it, then it's best for you to stay quiet."

Outraged, angry, and perturbed, you finally hung up on her. She had no empathy for you, your sisters, or anyone else her brother had harmed. All she cared about was protecting him. She had a clear motive for her call: to force you to pressure your sisters to keep their mouths shut and to threaten you to keep yours shut, too. Otherwise, Sohna would leave you. Since when did she care for your well being?

Instantly after you hung up, you were on your knees crying hysterically on your living room floor, keeled over like a child feeling sick and nauseous. You had no control over yourself or your emotions. Anger, rage, overwhelm, sadness, grief, pain, hurt, and trauma had all unleashed themselves inside your core at once. Your feelings were over the top; they consumed you, swallowing you whole and taking over all of you. It was as if something huge and terrifying was trying to release from inside you. It was coming from your entire body, from every cell, through every organ, up your chest, through your throat, and out your mouth. Like the horrid dark, gooey gunk that comes out of the clogged bathroom sink. It was invisible yet visible to you in an unexplainable way. It was coming out from inside of every pore and orifice of your body.

Something very profoundly strange happened to you. You were crying and rocking uncontrollably like a child. You were a child, alone, traumatized, and so distraught.

A child who had just been raped.

You, Jeeti, at that very moment were the child who had just realized a horrific truth: You were raped at 11 years old in your family living room back in October 1980. Now 37 years old, you had never gone back into your mind to acknowledge the first time Manjit raped you. All those years you had shut yourself off from that moment. You hadn't acknowledged it as rape. You had always thought you had something to do with it. You believed it was your fault, and in some way, you were to blame. But at that very moment, you faced it all.

The first time,
The second time,
The third time,
The rapes countless times after that.

You finally realized you had nothing to do with what Manjit had done to you. You didn't ask for it, provoke it, or do anything to deserve it. Of course, you enjoyed the attention he gave you when you were 11. You liked the feeling of being special. What child wouldn't? But that definitely didn't warrant rape. There on the living room floor you finally realized that being raped wasn't your fault; you weren't to blame.

You'd had it all wrong in your mind. In your younger years, you had sympathy for him rather than yourself. You now understood how you were conned, manipulated, used, and tortured for years. Your body was trying to release the emotional, physical, and psychological trauma it had suffered and suppressed for more than 25 years. You lay crying on the floor in a fetal position, loud painful sounds you never knew existed inside you now bursting out of you. Like an open faucet, tears flowed down your face as the molten lava from the pain and trauma of abuse locked deep inside erupted and exploded, scorching your entire being.

You didn't know it, but you had regressed into the 11-year-old Little Jeeti.

A little while later the phone rang. It was your friend Taj. She heard your shaken voice and came over immediately. She had never heard or seen you in this state before. Your sister Salakshana happened to call, and she soon followed, too. Taj tried to soothe you. Salakshana hugged you and cried. You finally calmed down a little. Curled up on the sofa, you would break out in bouts of tears uncontrollably. Like huge tidal waves, the emotions would rise and fall, smashing you and then washing through you. Out of the blue your cousin Babbu called; she could not believe what Parm was saying. She wanted to rip Parm's hair out of her head. Kira, your confidant, was away for work. Sohna was out running errands for the construction of your new dream house.

You began to calm a little on the sofa with the comfort of your sister and friend. It was a very bright, sunny Saturday afternoon, but not even the warm loving rays of the sun could soothe you. You knew the time had come to tell the man you loved the most about your horrible past. You had to tell Sohna the dark dreaded secret you thought you would take to your grave.

It was a few hours after Parm's phone call when Sohna came home. One look at you and he knew you were distraught.

"What's wrong?" he asked.

His eyes sought an answer looking at you, then Salakshana and Taj. You got up from the sofa and walked toward him. He hugged you immediately. You knew the time had come. You were going to break your silence no matter the cost. You couldn't have stopped yourself from telling him even if you wanted to. The knowingness inside you was loud and clear. It was time to tell Sohna the truth.

You both went upstairs into your bedroom. Sohna sat on the bed, and you sat in front of him, not knowing how he would react or take in the truth. You bowed your head to the truth and surrendered to its benevolent power, letting it flow off of your lips as if you were being released from the deadly curse of silence. You wasted no time in telling him the truth no matter how hard it was for you to convey or for him to hear. You did not hold back anything. It was important for you to finally speak your whole truth to someone you loved and trusted wholeheartedly, no matter your fate.

At that very moment everything stood still. It was as if the clock of life stopped ticking. Something inside of you had stopped. You just stopped running, from yourself, your past, your truth, and your story. You owned your truth. You had surrendered. All would be as it would be. You had let go of burying the secret.

The grave consequences of telling the truth did not matter. Consequences of losing the love of your life, your marriage, your precious little 6-year-old Maheema, the beautiful home, and life as you knew it. You didn't worry about your safety if Manjit would come after you. The only thing that mattered was the truth and your undying love for your husband and family.

Sohna hugged you as you cried. You were leaning into his chest, and he was lying on the bed leaning into the headboard. He had his arms around you, and with sincerity, he told you not to cry as he himself faced an internal hell of his own.

It was a while later when Salakshana came into your room. She was desperate to find out how you and Sohna were doing.

"Did it happen to you too?" Sohna asked her, looking right into her eyes.

She immediately flew into his arms. He hugged her as she cried and told him the truth. You left the room and gave both of them the privacy they deserved. You closed the door behind you not knowing what telling the truth had unleashed upon you, Sohna, your precious little Maheema, your sisters, and the entire family. Telling Sohna about being raped by Manjit was a life-changing decision for you. You didn't know how Sohna would react or if your bedroom door would be closed to you forever. You didn't know if Sohna would welcome you into his arms and your shared bed ever again. You walked away from your bedroom numb, frazzled, and scared. You walked away dissociated from yourself, not knowing standing up for the truth would empower you to a higher level of yourself.

With Love,

Jeeti

LETTER 15

You Are a Leader

Dear Jeeti,

You had seen it happen in many Hollywood movies, but you never thought it would happen to you. Yet there you were, crying in the middle of the grocery store aisle the very next day.

It was Sunday, a day after Parm's degrading phone call. Your cell phone rang, and it was Kira. She had finished her trip and called you the moment she landed at the Toronto airport. Kira was a flight attendant working for a Canadian airline, and you had a ritual where she would call you from the Toronto airport the minute she came back from her work from around the world.

"Hello," she said, tired and excited.

Your eyes watered the minute you heard your sister's voice. You tried to swallow your tears as she talked, choking your own voice. You didn't want to dump your pain and grief on her. That was not your style.

"What's wrong?" she asked.

Like a dam, a big lump sat in your throat holding back your sobs and tears and preventing you from answering her. The lump gave way as the tears broke free and streamed down your face. You couldn't control them anymore. The items on the shelf became a big blur with all the colourful packaging melting into one obscure dishevelled whole. You cried in the middle of the grocery store as you briefly told Kira about Parm's phone call. You started walking around the aisles like a zombie with your grocery basket in hand and Maheema following you. You were a few steps ahead and didn't want Maheema to see you cry. It would be too much for a six-year-old to bear. You wanted to shield her from your trauma.

"I'm going to Williams Lake in the morning to tell Mom and Dad," you told Kira as you circled the aisles. "I want them to hear what happened to me. They need to hear my truth, not lies from someone else. Jesse said he would drive me down."

You had made up your mind. The time had come for them to hear what Manjit had done to you. You gave no thought to what your parents and the rest of the family would think, do, or say to you. You were ready to walk into the wrath of your Edmonton family, too, all of whom were Manjit's brother and sisters. You were prepared to confront them all about what Manjit had done. You did not think about the consequences that had kept you muzzled—whether you would be blamed, further shunned, or outcasted from the family. Your focus was on telling them the truth.

Kira was fuming at what Parm had said. Since it was Sunday, there was no late night or red eye flight out of Toronto at that time with her company.

"I'm going to come, too. I should be able to make the first flight out in the morning," she said.

You got yourself together, went home, prepared dinner, and made enough for Sohna and Maheema to eat for the next day while you were gone. Your motherly and household duties continued despite your numb, emotional, and traumatized state.

Later that evening, Salakshana decided she would come along with you too. Your sister, Rakhee, too was able to miraculously fly in from the East Coast. The Universe had worked its wonders, and without any planning, somehow it all worked out that all of you siblings would be making the six-hour drive to Williams Lake in the morning. The timing and how it all came together was perfect.

By the next day, you all were sitting in the living room of your parents' house in Williams Lake. You had just arrived from Surrey that afternoon right before Dad and Uncle came home from work. It was Monday, September 11, 2006, and it had been two days since Parm's upsetting phone call. Dad sat beside Mom and Uncle sat down beside your Massi with their tea cups for their daily late afternoon tea.

You were there to tell them something. They knew you children must have come spontaneously for a good reason. They knew your brother Jesse wouldn't drive down all of his sisters for nothing. Your cousin, Babbu, had also driven from her hometown an hour away to support you and to let Mom and Dad know Manjit had touched her in a sexually inappropriate manner, too.

Your Massi got up and left at the start of the conversation, just like she had done 14 years earlier. She didn't want to listen or have anything to do with it. You confessed of all the sexual abuse you had suffered at the hands of Pago, Parmar, Papa, and Priest. You confessed that Manjit had raped and sexually assaulted you since you were 11 years old. Your sisters Salakshana and Kira, and your cousin Babbu, confirmed their suffering at the hands of Manjit, too. Just like that, it was all out in the open.

The painful truth was hard to hear. Dad sat on the sofa, shoulders slumped with one hand on his bowed head. None of us went into the full details of the abuse. Uttering the simple truth about having been sexually violated by Manjit was enough. Dad looked up a few times with tears in his eyes. He was trying to grasp the magnitude of what he was hearing. He was trying to process the information he had just received. Uncle cried, too. Mom sat quietly sobbing off and on. Your Massi had, on her own accord, decided to come back and had taken a seat by Uncle halfway through the conversation. Dad decided to call Masser in Edmonton to tell him what we disclosed.

"Hale te ithe di pund khul hi hai. Aje hathe di pund khulani hai," Dad said, meaning, *"It's only the pile of girls that have come out here and the pile there have yet to come out."*

Masser responded by saying, "Gunigaar bakshia nahi jana," meaning, *"The culprit will not be spared."*

You completely lost it when you thought of the magnitude of it all—the possibility of other little cousins having been potentially abused in your family. Somehow that thought hadn't entered your mind yet. You ended up wailing on the living room floor. One of your sisters and Uncle rushed to soothe you.

"I am here, I am here for you, okay," said Uncle.

His strong, muscular grip had never held you so tightly before. It felt safe, reassuring, and full of love. In that tender moment, he saw your innocence.

Someone will hold Manjit accountable, you thought.

Dad had asked for a sit down with Masser and Manjit. In the Punjabi culture, elders sit down to discuss the wrong and disagreements among family members to come to some sort of a resolution. Manjit would be asked to attend and take responsibility for what he had done. Dad would take a couple of his trusted friends and Uncle and sit down with Masser, Manjit, and his brothers-in-law (the husbands of Masser and Manjit's sisters). Mom, you, and your sisters would be present and most likely Manjit's sisters would show up, too. You would be able to confront him. Masser said he would talk to Manjit and arrange a sit down. He was going to call Dad back in a few days.

The news shook the Pooni household to its core. Everyone was filled with an array of emotions that night. No one in the house slept much. The following day, you all left back to Surrey. There was so much uneasiness inside you. It followed you all the way back to your home.

Your brain was constantly engaged in its natural fight, flight, or freeze response—a primitive survival instinct programmed in our bodies designed to protect a person when they perceive a harmful event, attack, or threat to survival. Your brain was drugged out from the overproduction of stress hormones and other chemical messengers (neurotransmitters) that had naturally invaded your body. Your mind was foggy, numb, and distant. You were completely stressed, dissociated from yourself, and knew you were not emotionally well.

Jeeti, you were still in a state of shock.

And you did not like feeling this way. You knew you had to get your head together. You knew you would need help to get back to your "normal" state, and you wanted to get there quickly for your daughter.

When you came back from Williams Lake, you picked up the phone to solicit the help of Dr. Alexander Lees. Kira had recommended him, as she had seen him herself and loved how he wasn't a conventional therapist. You had never seen a therapist and had no clue what talking to a stranger about your being sexually abused would be like.

Your first visit with Dr. Lees was about him getting to know you and what was bothering you. He had a large office on the first floor of his house. You had the choice of sitting on a sofa or a comfy chair. The sofa set reminded you of the old floral 80's patterned cream and brown velour sofa Dad had bought in Williams Lake, when you were 16. There was a cream blanket sitting on the sofa. Dr. Lees sat in his therapist's chair while you took your seat on the sofa. You were wrapped in your shawl, something you wore not only to keep you warm but also because it made you feel secure and protected. It felt weird and strange for you to sit in a therapist's office. It was difficult for the words "sexual abuse" and "rape" to roll off your tongue as you gave him a brief history of your past. You did not go into detail nor did he ask you to. The session felt somewhat awkward; it was the first time you were sharing tidbits of horror from your past with a therapist. The experience felt strange, and you didn't know what to make of your first session. Somehow, you knew to trust—to trust the process, trust this man, and trust that the healing would unfold.

You left the first session knowing you would be back for more. After that you saw Dr. Lees weekly. Therapy was costly, but you knew cost was not something you could worry about. Your sisters would help out without question, and if need be, you could ask your parents. You had to get help no matter how expensive it was. Many times, you booked two-hour sessions because an hour always flew by so quickly. You wanted to waste no time being emotionally and mentally unhealthy.

You really liked Dr. Lees. You fell in love with his methods and techniques of therapy and his use of humour. He was a well-experienced psychotherapist who helped clients overcome trauma, anxiety, and much more. He knew all about the cutting edge research on the mind and body connection and used unconventional methods, NLP (Neuro-Linguistic Programming), Time Line Therapy, guided imagery techniques involving making images and movie clips in your mind, anchoring, EFT (a tapping technique), and much more to help relieve your stress, trauma, anxiety, and all the things you were experiencing. From the very first moment you walked into his office, Dr. Lees helped you start your healing process. With his support you started to deal with the carnage left behind by the ruthless tornado that had ripped through your life.

He helped you start the process of transforming and integrating the trauma encrypted in every cell of your body. You were fascinated by his words. He could talk from his personal experience and knew about the non-physical mind and its tremendous effects in the physical world. You embraced his techniques that enabled you to begin (in baby steps) the letting go process and the releasing of the weight, pain, trauma, and fears of memories from your past. You were able to bring to the surface some of your old limiting beliefs and patterns. These were things you didn't know existed in you before then. You saw Dr. Lees off and on for more than 10 years until he passed away in January of 2016. Your journey to healing would not have been possible without him.

Sadly, that journey didn't come easy. About a month after Parm's phone call, you started to realize there would be no sit down of the elders. All the adults chose to remain quiet. None of them mentioned the words "sit down" again.

Uncle started saying to you, "He (Manjit) is going to say you were the one coming to him. What will you do then? What will you say? There is nothing you can do. Nothing."

Just like that, he took Manjit off the hook by turning it around on you. It became very clear to you that your Dad, Mom, Uncle, Masser, and Edmonton family were not going to do anything about holding Manjit accountable. It was as if they were scared. As if they had their own demons to hide. Neither Dad, Mom, nor Uncle questioned Manjit. Forget about a sit down, they didn't even make a phone call to him! They threw in the towel without making any attempt to even ask Manjit how he had the nerve to do what he did.

"I'm ready to call the police," you told Kira six months later in March 2007.

You had already called your victim support worker assigned by the Surrey Women's Center who would support you through this process. She was to arrive any minute.

"I am going to call them today. It's okay if you don't want to do this today, but I am going to," you told Kira.

Kira lived with you now and would be home off work for a few weeks. Your home was her home. Throughout life, you always looked for support in each other—the kind of support that wouldn't come from anyone else.

"Go ahead. I'm in," she said.

You had asked Salakshana to come over as well but did not mention you had called the police. You told her when she arrived and gave her space to make her own choice. Seeing you and Kira survive giving your initial complaint to the police officer first would give Salakshana courage to do the same. The officer came to the house a couple of hours later. He took your complaints and said he would be in touch for formal police interviews at the police station.

Thus, the saga of holding Manjit accountable through the criminal justice system began.

So did the name Kuta (*pronounced Koo-ta*), a name you had heard your Mom, Massis, and Bollywood actresses use towards males, meaning a *"male dog."* It's similar to the derogatory word "bitch" which refers to a female. It was hard for you to call him Manjit; the name would not roll off your tongue. It was easier to refer to him as the Kuta. Everyone would instantly know who you were talking about.

In August of 2007, almost a year after Parm's phone call and four months after your initial police complaint, you and your sisters were preparing for a younger cousin's wedding in Edmonton. He was your Massi and Masser in Edmonton's son, and you adored him. This younger cousin had told Kira that he would talk to his Dad (Masser) about not inviting the Kuta (who was his uncle) to his wedding. It was about three weeks before the wedding when you learned the Kuta was also invited. You, Kira, and Salakshana decided you were not going to the wedding. You wanted to have nothing to do with people who supported a rapist and included him in family functions after knowing full well what he had done, brushing everything under the carpet.

You would get rid of people from your life that had no respect or dignity for little girls and showed no concern for their safety, even if they were people you loved.

You would stand your ground and not cave to the fingers of blame and shame that pointed your way.

You would not crumble to the narrow minds of those in the Kuta's family that said, "It could not even be 1% true Manjit did anything to the Pooni girls."

You would dismiss those in your family that said, "Jeeti should have known better. Why did she keep on going back?"

You would cut out the ones who claimed, "Salakshana was older. How could it happen to her? She should have known better."

You deafened your ears to those that said, "It was you who was going to him and wanted him."

Their ignorance prevented them from seeing you and your sisters as little girls. They blamed you, Jeeti. Instead of focusing their energy on protecting others, they chose to waste their breath on blaming and discrediting you.

Mom and Dad had a lot to think about, too. On one hand, culturally they had to think about what people would say if they didn't go to the wedding. On the other hand, they had to think about their daughters. Who would they support? The decision did not come easily. It was important for Dad to be a good uncle, and he had genuine love for his extended family. But Mom and Dad knew if they chose to attend the wedding, they would risk losing their daughters. So, they decided not to go.

When Masser learned your parents were not going to the wedding, he called Dad, trying desperately to convince him. He told Dad to come by himself and to forget the girls. Dad called you and had some not very nice things to say to you.

"You were the one who always sat beside him," he said in anger. "You didn't listen. You didn't stop."

He too laid the blame on you. You were distraught. You had hoped your Dad would understand. In your mind you didn't get why he would even entertain the thought of going to this wedding or why he would be having conversations with family members who clearly did not support his daughters. He didn't owe them anything. After all, he was the one who helped them all come to Canada. He was the one who gave them his love and support. You listened to him on the other end of the phone like a wounded little girl doused in shame, feeling not good enough, disappointed in yourself, dirty, and at fault.

You defended yourself and voiced your frustration to Dad. He just didn't get it. He too couldn't empathize with you. You questioned in your mind whether he ever loved you. Why did no one care about you and what was done to you? Why did everyone blame you and think you were so horrible when all you wanted was to do good? All you wanted was to protect your little princess and other girls like her. What blinders did they all have on? What lens were they living life through?

After the conversation, along with your tears, you brushed away your father's hurtful words. Your Dad's older sister (the Kuta and Masser's mom) also called from India to try and convince Dad to go. She hadn't called him for years and was now calling to ask him to "put water under the bridge and let bygones be bygones." She offered no compassion or apology to Dad for her son's actions. Instead, she insisted he go to the wedding.

In the end, Mom and Dad did not go. Your Uncle and Massi in Williams Lake—your lifelong second set of parents—and their children decided to go. That was the end of your relationship with them.

Unlike the elders in your life—the ones you had once looked up to, held in such high regard, put on a pedestal, respected, and loved unconditionally—you did not cower to shame, humility, and ignorance. You had no role model in your family or in your brown culture to look up to. There was no leader to follow.

Now, Jeeti, you were taking the lead.

Without knowing it, you were setting a precedent. You stood up like a mighty pillar and took your post ready for battle. You were using your voice and truth as your sword and armour. You were ready to defend Little Jeeti, Salakshana, Kira, Babbu, and others.

You were ready to put a stop to the Kuta once and for all.

With Love,

Jeeti

PART FOUR

Awaken

LETTER 16

Precious Innocent Princess

Dear Maheema,

Your dad and I were blessed with you in April 2000. Our precious baby girl, princess Maheema.

Your dad and I had lived happily, dancing as lovers to the joy of life. You came 3 1/2 years into our marriage when I was 31 years old. You were perfect with big brown eyes, long tiny fingers, a round head, very little brown hair, the cutest smile, and the best newborn baby smell. You were sweet and innocent. Your dad named you, and together, we were in awe of your every first—the first cry, smile, giggle, tooth, step, word, and more.

My family was super excited, too. Your Salakshana Massi, Kira Massi, Rakhee Massi, and your cousin Chandani were all elated and so happy to find out you were a baby girl. They had wanted a girl; the boys in my family were spoiled brats. The last baby my family had was Chandani, a girl, who was almost 14 years old when you were born. Your aunts and uncles in your dad's family were equally excited. Your dad and I didn't know if we were having a girl or a boy, and we didn't mind either. All we wanted was a baby. I wanted it to be a complete surprise when you would pop out into this world. I wanted to give you all the love in the world whether you were a girl or a boy.

You were our first baby. A baby both your dad and I had longed for. A baby we were so happy to have. We had been trying to conceive for a while before you came. We were so delighted to have you, a baby girl and our precious princess.

Becoming a mother opened up an entire ocean of love in my heart. I was a very loving person as it was, but motherhood expanded limitless love into my being. Along with wearing the hat of a wife, loving sister, and business woman, I now also wore the hat of a proud mother. I wore that hat with pride. Both your dad and I gave you so much love, affection, and protection. You were a daddy's girl. He could never say no to you.

Four months after you were born, I saw the Kuta up close again.

I hadn't seen him up close for years. He had remarried by then. Of course, I did not plan to see the Kuta. I did not know Mom had invited him to my brother Jesse's engagement party in Williams Lake. Yes, the same mother who had wanted to invite Parmar and his family to my wedding four years earlier even though I had told her what Parmar had done to me.

"He can sit in the Gurdwara where all the others will sit. You won't even notice him," she had said.

In the end, she didn't invite Parmar to my wedding.

Maheema, you were all dolled up that day, wearing tiny red bangles and a bindi on your forehead. I was holding you in my arms when I got up to welcome the large number of guests arriving from Edmonton. I failed to see the Kuta in the group until he was coming toward me.

"She is so cute," he said, reaching to touch your little arm.

An electrical shock ran through me when he touched you, my little princess. It was as if I had been electrocuted. I hugged you tightly and quickly moved you away from him. I was so uncomfortable with him touching you. An alarm had gone off in my body sensing danger, and it was my instinct to protect you from him.

As you grew, I became hypersensitive to where my hands rested on you. I would move my hand if it rested on your round baby bum. I was incredibly aware every time I cleaned your private parts. I would become scared as I watched you, my little baby, sleep flat on your back in your crib with legs spread open. You looked so innocent and so vulnerable. A strange sense of fear was heightened inside of me after having you. When I used to come into your room in the middle of the night to feed you, my fear would be at an all-time high. As I fed you, scary thoughts of someone being in the room or coming after us would come into my mind, just like they did when I was a little girl. I would hold you tight, rock you back and forth, and attempt to protect you from the danger that I was perceiving in my mind.

You were just six years old when I broke my silence and told the truth about the Kuta. Having you, my precious princess, had a lot to do with me breaking my silence. He was at every family function in Edmonton, and your Kira Massi and I always made sure you were protected. It felt absurd to us that no one was watching him. I wanted to protect you from him. I wanted to ensure his evilness would not make its way to you. I didn't want him to harm you in any way. I did not want him to look at you in the evil, lustful way he had looked at me. I did not want him around you at all. I did not want him to be able to secretly admire you, fantasize of you, think of what he would do to you with his fingers or penis. I didn't want him to have thoughts about how he would undress you and rape you. I didn't want him to think about the pleasure he could reap from your body. I could not have him look at your innocent girly curves, your undeveloped bosom, the roundness of your buttocks, or your strong thighs as an invitation for him to violate you. I could not have him misread your innocent facial gestures or the look in your big brown eyes as signals of desire for him. He was sick—a sick diseased Kuta—and I had to stop him dead in his tracks. I could not let the cycle of abuse continue.

Maheema, having you in my life when Parm's nasty phone call

came helped me see myself as the Little Jeeti that I was when I had first been raped. It helped me see my sisters as little girls, too. Your presence helped me see Little Jeeti as a little princess, just like you. It made me realize Little Jeeti was someone's daughter, too. She was someone's precious little darling just like you. Raising you through all your growth stages and having a girl child in my life opened my eyes and my love for all the other young girls the Kuta had hurt. Being a mother to you and watching you dance and twirl in a chunni just like I had strengthened my resolve to do my best to stop this man from harming others.

Suing him in civil court for his money was not the path I wanted to take. I wanted someone to stop him from harming others, and in my mind, the only one who could do that was the police. So, I chose to hold him accountable in criminal court where he would have to answer to the police, face the court, be sentenced, jailed, and have a criminal record so others could be warned and remain safe. I wanted to see him have no possible way to harm other girls.

So, in 2007, after my parents and family failed to hold the Kuta accountable, I went to the mighty force of the Royal Canadian Mounted Police (RCMP), thinking they could stop him from harming someone else and hold him responsible for what he had done. I gave them my formal statement and so did your Kira Massi, Salakshana Massi, and later my cousin Babbu. How was I able to do that? Because of you, Maheema. Having a girl child gave me courage to stand up and take steps forward in stopping the Kuta. Maheema, you have no idea the impact you had on my moving forward and dealing with the Kuta and my sexual abuse. I couldn't have done it without you.

For years my police complaint file sat as a historical sexual abuse file collecting dust in the RCMP station at Williams Lake. I was bounced from one police officer to another. All the while, I did my best to make life as normal for you while I was dealing with the whole ordeal. I hid my pain from you and did my best to be a present parent for you. Your Kira Massi, Salakshana Massi, cousin Chandani, and your dad were your best playmates. I joined in the fun, too, whenever I could, my favourite activity being our water fights where we soaked your dad. I loved it when we turned the sprinkler on underneath the trampoline and jumped on it as the water moved from one side to the other, making us all wet and cool in the hot summer sun. I watched you and your body grow in your complete innocence. I ensured every day you were surrounded by immense love and safety.

You were so precious to me, my princess Maheema.

As you grew, so did the dust on my police file. Every few months or so, I would call or email the RCMP to inquire if someone had looked into my case file. During this time I continued to see Dr. Lees. I had to ensure my emotional and mental health was taken care of so I could take care of you, myself, our family, and my fashion business. I also had to ensure I held on to my courage to keep on messaging the RCMP as I was tossed from one officer to the next. Little did I know it would be more than three years before an RCMP constable (a woman herself) would remove the dust and cobwebs off my case file and finally pay attention to the horror inside.

Many times in those years I saw Little Jeeti in you. Sometimes it was your hair, sometimes it was your face and your expressions, sometimes it was your body, and many times it was your innocence. Every year when you turned a different age, I compared myself, Little Jeeti, to you. I thought about how small and innocent Little Jeeti was when she was sexually abused by one person and then the next. Every year, looking at you, I would think, *Oh, this is how old I was when I was touched. This is how small I was, and that is what my innocent little girly curves looked like. I too must have been so purely innocent. How could someone do something like that? How could someone hurt an innocent little child? How sick and evil that person must be!*

I used to think about how one day you would have an 11th

birthday. I wondered if that would be difficult on me because I was raped by the Kuta when I was 11. Tears would roll down my face just at the thought of it.

Maheema, you were eight years old when we gave you the news that I was pregnant. You were so happy. You had asked me numerous times over the years, "Mommy, when are we going to have a baby?" Your friends' moms were pregnant at school. They had siblings, and you wanted one, too. It was a long wait to grow our family. It was a miracle we finally conceived again.

I first felt the baby flutter in my stomach during our trip to Hawaii with you and your Kira Massi. I remember the exact moment. It was when you and I were riding the waves at Waikiki. You and I did this for hours. We went deeper into the ocean until your feet didn't touch the ground. You clung to me; you trusted me. I'd jump up with you and land on my feet, holding you above the water. The baby would flutter inside my stomach the whole time, as if the three of us were in unison. It was as if we were all one, experiencing joy, love, and excitement together.

In April 2009, we were blessed with another little princess, your sister Shia. You were nine years old and so proud to be a big sister. You fed her, changed her, and rocked her. Your wish of having a sister had come true, and I was so glad because I wanted you to have a sister. I knew the importance of having a sister firsthand. Given my age, I knew your dad and I were not going to have another baby even though I had always wanted three children. I was 40 when I had Shia, and she was the last one to come.

With Shia, the same uncomfortable feeling crept into my body when I watched her laying in the crib, so innocent and vulnerable. Like you, she was so peaceful, her chest rising and falling as she drifted to sleep. Unfortunately, I did not feel that same peace. I felt fear at just the sight of her. I couldn't watch how vulnerable she was because I knew it was my job to protect her—to protect you both—from being torn apart by someone evil. What if I somehow fail to do so?

With her too, I watched where my hand rested on her body as I cleaned her soiled diaper or bathed her. That was the most frightening feeling for me—the fear of touching her body in the wrong way. This fear was much more intense with her than it was with you. I wasn't able to enjoy touching both of my little girls the way a mother is biologically designed to do. It was another thing the Kuta took from me.

Perhaps the increase in fear and anxiety when Shia was born came because I had broken my silence. I was dealing with the whole ordeal of holding the Kuta accountable when she was born. Because of that, I was always on guard. Thoughts flooded my mind that I may be an abuser myself for feeling so uncomfortable around your little bodies. Consciously, I never believed I would do anything wrong. I knew I would never hurt either of my girls, but I couldn't get the thoughts out of my mind.

"It's called being hypersensitive," Dr. Lees told me when I shared this with him. "Those that have been sexually abused become hypersensitive to touch, whether you are touching someone or someone is touching you. So, you are more aware of where your hand rests and how you clean private parts than a mother who hasn't experienced sexual abuse. She wouldn't think anything of it at all."

I loved being enlightened by Dr. Lees. He always knew how to reframe something so I could see it for what it really was. What seemed so scary and complicated to me was explained in a way I could totally understand. Over time, he helped free me from these fears so that I could love parenting you and Shia in every single way.

Maheema, as you and Shia have both grown, I have seen so much of my sisters and I in you both when we were little. When you hug, cuddle, tickle, giggle, tease, and fight with each other, it reminds me of my sisters. When Shia pulls your hair, or you both horse around, or you give each other unconditional love, it reminds me of us. It reminds me how Little Jeeti, Little Kira, and

Little Salakshana once were. It helps me remember that we too deserved and needed protection. Watching you two grow allowed me to have a deeper connection with Little Jeeti. It allowed me to fully see Little Kira and Little Salakshana in their vibrancy and innocence. It allowed me to love those little girls in myself and my sisters.

Birthing and raising you two opened my eyes to all the other little girls in the world that deserved to be safe and protected. Being a mother of two little girls sealed my destiny to follow only one path.

The path of standing up for myself and using my voice to speak my truth.
The path of protecting you two.
The path of accountability and justice.
The path that would only move forward.
The path that needed to be taken without question.
The path that was unknown by any woman I knew.
The path I would have to pave myself with an end I could not predict.

No matter the consequence, I ventured onto this path with my head held high. It is you two and Little Jeeti that beat that drum for me. You, Maheema, helped me move forward.

There was no turning back.

With Love,

Your Mommy

Jeeti

LETTER 17

Trust the Synchronocities

Dear Shia,

You had problems latching when you were born and couldn't feed properly. I won't get into my feelings about the old nurse at the hospital who told me not to feed you for eight hours so that eventually you would get hungry and feed. You ended up back at the hospital a day after we brought you home. You weren't getting enough breast milk and had become jaundiced. You had no energy to suck milk from my breast or a bottle, and you would fall asleep and stay asleep every time I tried to feed you. It was scary to watch you for four days under the blue bili-light in a baby incubator with a feeding tube going through your nose. You were so tiny and so precious. Your dad, Maheema, and I had waited nine years for you to come into this world. You had wanted to come hours earlier, but despite my concerns, the overnight nurse overlooked that my extremely full bladder was blocking the natural unfolding of the birthing process.

It wasn't only the complications at birth that made those days difficult. You came into this world with pain, trauma, and suffering all passed down to you through our family of origin or endured in some past lifetime. The horrific details you recounted at 2 1/2 years old proved so. I had seen an episode of Dr. Oz's show where he shared research on how trauma can be passed down from generation to generation in a family. He talked about a study in which mice were electrically shocked when the scent of cherry blossoms was released into the air. According to the study, the offspring of the mice (three generations worth!) were also afraid of the cherry blossom smell even though they hadn't been shocked. I knew all those months you were in the womb it wasn't just the beliefs, feelings, and trauma held in my body that were passed down to you; through epigenetics, it was also the beliefs, emotions, and trauma held by your grandmothers, great-grandmothers, and generations back down our family line that too had been passed down to you.

You were 2 years old when I finally received the long-awaited news. Almost 4 years after my initial RCMP police report, the Kuta was finally arrested and charged on September 1, 2011. He was held on six counts of sexual assault pertaining to me, Salakshana, Kira, and my cousin Babbu. Little did I know this was only just the beginning of the journey up my personal Mt. Everest—a journey the likes of which no one had ever tread before.

Two years after his arrest, we finally had our preliminary hearing at the Provincial Court of British Columbia in our hometown of Williams Lake. Your Massis and I were like deer caught in headlights during that preliminary hearing. The details of the entire court saga I will save for future writings—rich insightful details to be bound and shared in a book of its own on the horrors that lie in pursuing justice through the Canadian criminal justice system. The whole ordeal was like a poorly written, neverending Bollywood movie full of one defence delay tactic after another. It was a brutal process.

It was after that initial hearing that the court case became much bigger. It began as something only about me, my sisters, my daughters, and my family, but then, it became about a much bigger cause: to stand up for the most vulnerable in my culture and for all survivors who would find themselves in the criminal justice system. The preliminary hearing was such a dysfunctional process and going through it ignited anger and fire in me. I had to do something to help others who might one day be in the same position.

I started to record some personal thoughts on my camcorder to capture some of what I was going through. These were moments I knew I could use in a documentary one day. You see, Shia, ever since I had broken my silence back in September 2006, I had this desire to make a documentary on the sexual abuse I experienced in my life and knew how important it was to do so. I knew sexual abuse wasn't just my story; it was the story of countless others in my culture. Over centuries, it was a deep, buried secret no one dared to talk about. There were so many others suffering in silence, and it was time for someone to speak up. I did not know how I was going to do it; I only knew that I would.

The whispers started coming from a deep place inside, saying, *"Make a documentary. Make a documentary."* The whispers, the voice, the nudging coming from within did not come from my sisters, family, friend, another human being, or even my own mind. They were coming from a much deeper place in my core. Shia, I followed those whispers—the knowingness that came from within. I had not yet recognized it as my loyal, trusting companion. But in reality, the voice within was no stranger to me. Following it had led me to monumental moments in my life: freeing myself from the Kuta, marrying the love of my life, having my two girls, starting my fashion design business, standing in my truth, breaking my silence, and discovering Little Jeeti and her innocence. The knowingness led me to these places, and I knew following it now would lead me again.

The story of how it all actually came to be is quite remarkable.

It started, way before I broke my silence when I first wrote down the name Selwyn Jacob after watching him speak at the screening of *Bollywood Bound*, a National Film Board of Canada (NFB) produced documentary. Selwyn was a producer at the NFB, and I had written down his name as a person to approach when I was ready to make a documentary of my own. Back then, I was a fashion designer and thought I was going to make a film on my gifted capabilities creating exquisite designs that incorporated the fusion of eastern fabrics, patterns, and embroideries with western silhouettes. No one (not even myself!) would ever have guessed back then what the documentary would ultimately be about. Sexual abuse, rape, and incest—they're all taboo subjects in our brown culture and words no one dared to even whisper. Back then, I would've never dared consider making this the subject of my film. I never expected there would ever come a day I would break my silence.

A year later, I met Baljit Sangra, a producer of a local TV show who had invited me to appear on her show. I would meet with Baljit once every few years as she produced her first documentary, *Warrior Boys*. I had hoped to gain insight on how I could make my own documentary on my personal story of sexual abuse. She was kind and easy to talk to. Over time, I formed with Baljit something that did not come very easy for me: trust. I was never the type to have a huge social circle. I usually kept to myself. But somehow, I felt I could trust Baljit.

Nearly a year after the traumatizing preliminary hearing, I met a woman at the Los Angeles airport. I was in the area for business in regards to my couture shawl collection, and there at the airport, I found myself drawn to this white woman. She was tall and slender with a nice smile, shoulder length hair, and a sweetness to her. We engaged in a friendly conversation as we waited at the gate to board our flight. To my surprise, she was a documentary producer! I soaked in every word as she spoke passionately about her film project. Her name was Gillian Darling Kovanic. We only had a few minutes to chat, but as we were boarding, I shared with her my desire to make a documentary on my personal story of sexual abuse. She gave me her contact information and told me she lived off an island near Vancouver.

That next month, I set up a meeting with both Selwyn and Gillian. I met with Selwyn first, placing the one-page story of my life in front of him and telling him I wanted to make a documentary incorporating my personal story. As he read, I tried to read him, watching his body language, his reaction, and his fingers rubbing his forehead. He nodded his head slowly as he gazed out the window in deep thought. When he finally spoke, he mentioned how unheard of it was for a subject (like myself) to approach the film board to make a documentary. It's usually a producer or director that comes up with the subject matter and finds participants to film and share their story.

I smiled in response. Yes, this was rare, but so was I.

He didn't promise me anything and said he would be in touch. I walked away from the meeting feeling optimistic. In my mind, I knew how big this project was and how badly the story needed to be told. I knew it would shake my family, my culture, and the entire Indian community. I also knew that if the NFB didn't take this project on, I would find another way to make the film. My mind was racing with creative ideas. I didn't know how, of course, but I was determined. I knew this film was going to be made. This story had to be told. It was long overdue.

The next day I met with Gillian. She was lovely, warm, and super supportive. To my surprise, she had previously worked for the NFB. She saw the importance of telling my story and told me to write a proposal as soon as possible. I had no idea what a documentary proposal was or even how to write one, but she gave me reassurance, built my confidence, and shared some tips. Suddenly, there I was, a person with no film experience writing a proposal to make a documentary. I completed the proposal in about a week's time and handed it to Selwyn. I trusted the synchronicities and felt the movement of energy inside me—the knowingness nudging me to make the documentary and communicating to me the time was now. It all felt exciting, inspiring, and scary.

I was very excited when the NFB accepted my proposal! A

year later, Baljit was brought on to the film as a director. The subject matter was sensitive, so it was important to have a director I could trust and open up to and who was from the same cultural background as myself. Baljit and I had already built a rapport—a friendship with each other—and I knew if I trusted her, my family would trust her, too. It is not easy to share intimate details of your life with someone. There was a part of me that questioned if I knew what I was doing by putting my trust in the NFB and Baljit. Still, I trusted the knowingness that came from inside and followed its guidance.

As my plans to create a documentary rolled along, so did the setting of repeated dates for the criminal trial in the Supreme Court of British Columbia in Williams Lake. After numerous defence adjournments, the Supreme Court trial scheduled for January 2015 finally started later in July 2015.

And so did the filming of the documentary that would be called *Because We Are Girls*.

With Love,

Your Mommy

Jeeti

LETTER 18

Expose the Intruder in the Shadows

Dear Sohna,

You will always be my beloved prince.

Never in my wildest dreams could I have ever imagined swimming the depths of the ocean of love and seeing the wonders of the world like I have with you. I can only imagine how difficult and painful it must have been for you to hear me tell you I was raped at 11 years old by the Kuta. I'm sure the torture of the sexual abuse I suffered at the hands of men was horrendous for you to hear, especially given your traditional upbringing and the cultural parameters around virginity, shame, and family honour.

Once I revealed my dark hidden secret to you, your eyes could not meet my gaze. For months my eyes sought answers from yours, thirsty with a deep hunger and desire to see if you still loved me and wanted me in your life. I was so afraid that what I'd find in your eyes would be an affirmation that I was a dirty, dishonest, filthy betrayer. Without you having to say a word, your eyes told your internal tale of pain and sorrow. Gone was the loving, magnificent green colour of your eyes. Now it was replaced by a deep, dark brown. It was something I had never seen before—you with dark, angry eyes that could cut through anything. You were struggling to comprehend and make sense of it all. You did not and could not reach out for help. You were angry, lost, and confused.

You were taught to deal with all your problems and keep them to yourself. How to deal with rape and sexual abuse was something that was never programmed into your brain or belief system by your family or culture. It was a subject never talked about, as if rape and sexual abuse don't exist in our culture. With no one to talk to and no outlet for release, you kept everything inside. You did not share any of your thoughts and feelings with me. You suffered in silence as you made an effort to wrap your head around the massive ordeal.

Culturally, you had a golden ticket out of our marriage. No one would blame you for leaving. It would be me, your wife, blamed for being impure, dishonourable, and a cheat. I would be blamed for being raped and sexually abused. I would be responsible for not being honest with you, especially since you had asked me about the Kuta years before we married. Certainly, words from your older brother's disapproval of accepting me into your family must have come down like a sledgehammer as you listened to me tell the horrific truth about my past.

You cannot marry her.
She is someone else's leftovers.
If you marry her, you cannot bring her into this house.

To this day, I do not know what made your brother believe I was a slut. It could have been Salakshana's ex-husband who said something bad about me to your brother back in the day. They were friends and kept in touch after the divorce. It could have been compounded by the fact that I was more influenced by the western culture. I was educated, confident, and independent. That would not fit into the hierarchy in your family and would dismantle the financial and familial control of your older brother. And yes, your family was traditional. An arranged marriage for you with a "good girl" from Punjab, India was what they had in mind for you.

"I'm leaving everything for you," you had said as you kneeled on one knee and took my hand the night before our wedding.

You and I had escaped from everyone's sight for a few minutes to have a moment of our own, leaving the pre-wedding festivities, family, and wedding guests behind. You and your guests had arrived at Williams Lake from Edmonton that evening. I felt like Juliet, dressed in my embroidered yellow dhoti Indian ensemble as I watched you from the balcony of my parent's house. I threw red roses your way as you walked up the long driveway to the mesmerizing beat of a live dhol played by your friend. You were too shy to look up. The large mirror work on my ensemble reflected rays of shimmering light your way, begging you to look. It was that night we had driven away from my parent's house, climbed a ladder onto the roof of a nearby school, and chosen to have our one-on-one moment.

This was your official proposal to me. My sisters had set it all up—the ladder, the champagne, the rose petals, and the blanket. Mother Nature had taken care of the moonlight and shining stars that sparkled above us that June night. Your face looked a little stressed in the moonlight, not from the 11-hour drive to Williams Lake but from the abandonment of your older brother and old Phua whom you loved and respected. Still, you held me in a tight lover's embrace. We kissed. You looked more handsome than ever. Your smile took my breath away. You kneeled and took my hand. Your eyes were full of love, pain, and sorrow, looking upward and locking into mine to seek reassurance that you were doing the right thing by marrying me. My heart felt your pain, and there, I vowed to be a good wife to you.

I knew how difficult the decision to marry me against your family's wishes was for you. I knew how agonizing the 5 years of waiting for them to come around had been.

I'm leaving everything for you.

Your words came with a lot of weight for the both of us.

After learning about the sexual abuse, your insides churned. I could only imagine the thoughts running through your head.

I can't believe I left my family for her.
How could she do this to me?
How could I be such a fool for believing her?
How did I not see it?
How can I ever believe anything she says again?
How can I trust her?
What else is she hiding from me?
What am I supposed to do now?
Do I stay or leave?
What about my child?
Where do I go now?
I brought this onto myself; my family warned me.
How will I ever be able to face them?

You must have felt so trapped. I could feel your shame, confusion, and anger. The waves kept smashing your being. Even though you didn't say much verbally, your lean stature carried so much shame. Shame in having been betrayed and deceived by your lover. Shame in being made a fool of. Shame in losing your family's honour. You must have thought about how I should have conveyed the truth to you a long time ago, back when we were dating. Then, you could have rightfully made the choice to marry me or not. The wounded look on your face and the heaviness you carried inside you said it all. Even though you did not convey your thoughts and feelings to me, your silence said so much.

Don't forget, my love, I too am Indian. I was raised in the same culture as you were, the culture that knows only to blame and shame the raped further. I was given the same knowledge of how our culture and the mind of an Indian male worked when it came to virginity, rape, sexual abuse, sex, and incest. I knew you too well. I knew the constrictions placed on your mind by our culture and the limiting beliefs you held. I knew you would not handle learning the truth about what the Kuta had done to me at any point in time.

And if I'm honest, it felt like once I conveyed the truth, you made it all about you. Feeling empathy for your lover—the wife and the Little Jeeti inside of her—seemed far from your mind. You were buried in your own pain and thoughts of deceit and betrayal. You were angry, and like most men who love their wives, you had the thought of wanting to kill the Kuta. But what good would that do? You would have to spend time in jail. How would that be justice? Our family would suffer. Your little girls would suffer. You and I would suffer.

Please know that I could never have told you the truth while we were dating. Not in a million years, my love. I was protecting myself and my very survival. The shame and humiliation of it all was so deep. I had been marinated in this shame and humiliation since I was a little girl. They were my best friends, my confidants, my blankets keeping me company day and night. To separate myself from them and have the courage to stand up for myself when I was a tender, young adult was unthinkable. Look at the catastrophe it reeked into our lives once I tore off the veil of shame and found courage to tell you the truth. Imagine the devastation that would have unfolded if I had mentioned a word of it to you back then. There would be no Sohna and Jeeti forever, no Maheema and Shia, no dancing of our souls as mad lovers into the next millennia.

Back then, I wouldn't have known what to tell you. I hadn't yet comprehended the magnitude of the Kuta's evil and what he had unleashed upon me. I didn't understand what grooming was. I hadn't even realized I was raped. No matter how much you loved me, your heart would not have been able to understand the psychological trauma, post-traumatic stress, or any other protective mechanism the human brain employs to survive. I didn't understand it myself. And if I had told you back then, you would have walked the other way. You would have simply left. The very same eyes that watched you gracefully prance into my life would have had to powerlessly watch you storm away. You were too young and naive back then to understand the vast cruelty the Kuta had inflicted upon me. You would have sought answers from your logical mind instead of an open, compassionate heart. The psychology of abuse, trauma, and its effects on humans is too complex to understand with the mind alone. You would have surrendered under the pressure of cultural beliefs and attitudes, too. Look how hard it was to wrap your head around it when you were much older and wiser. Like the rest of the world, you would have blamed me and branded me as the guilty one. Your love for me would have caved under the weight of shame, humiliation, and deception.

Many family members made bets in their minds, predicting that you would leave me and end our marriage when you learned of my history with the Kuta. Most men in our culture would not stick around in a marriage after that. Most men would rather not know to begin with. It takes a brave soul to work through a marriage filled with secrets of sexual abuse and rape.

My beloved, you are that brave soul, because you chose to stay.

Something about you was different from other Indian men in our Punjabi culture. Even though you may have contemplated it in your mind, not once did you ever talk about leaving. Slowly, the magnificent green colour of your eyes returned, as did your radiant smile. Daily, we picked up the pieces of our shattered selves and started walking forward together. For me the path forward was with you and my girls.

I had to flush out and expose the imposter who lurked in the shadows of my life in order to be rid of him forever. I had to expose the sexual violence inflicted by the Kuta not only on myself, but also on the other girls in my family. No matter which way I turned, his evil lurked, threatening to pounce out of the shadows from where it resided. To be done with it once and for all, I had to continue fighting to hold the Kuta accountable. It was a task, my elders, family members, and the criminal justice system had failed to do. After years of suffering and perseverance, my voice became loud, clear, and strong. I aspired to use that voice to bring light and attention to what girls and women face daily. I was compelled to shine light on the rape, incest, and sexual abuse that exists in our brown culture. I wanted to advocate for a change in the beliefs and mindsets that perpetuate and allow rape to flourish.

You see, my love, the obedience, oppression, and suppression of women and children in our culture allows it to be a breeding ground for pedophiles and rapists. It allows sexual abuse to perpetuate and the cycle to repeat generation after generation. It was my duty then and it is my duty now to stand up and speak my truth to stop the cycle of abuse in our family and advocate for change in our family and culture. I must be a voice for those who are not allowed to have one.

You wanted a simple, quiet, and private life. You did not want me to make the documentary and be in the eye of the public. I remember the day I told you I was going to make the film. I knew it was something I had to do for myself, whether you understood or not. The desire to make it was coming from a deep unexplainable place. I was not seeking permission from you; I was telling you and you knew that. I understood that I was risking our marriage in even bringing it up. We'd come so far, and yet still had such a distance to go.

"It's okay if you don't want to be with me anymore," I told you. "It's okay for you to go after the kind of life you desire. I know how difficult shouldering the entire financial burden has been on you. I would never force you to stay with me. I will love you no matter what."

The conversation was difficult to have, but it was necessary. My arms wanted to pull you toward me and hug you against my chest so your heart could understand the language of my soul. You felt so alone, with no one else to talk to and having to keep everything bottled up inside—as is the norm in our culture. My tears wanted to wash away your suffering. My love, it has been hard to watch you suffer as you have been dragged into this journey with me, and it indeed has been an excruciatingly long journey to find justice. I understand your frustration. I know my decision to make the documentary added another layer of pressure on you and what was already a long, painful criminal justice system journey.

You, my love, must have had many of the same concerns I had. I did consider but did not dwell upon the possibility that, when the story came out via the documentary, there would be those who wouldn't believe me. I would be ridiculed and further shamed by ruthless critics, bystanders, and those protecting the disgusting attitudes of men toward girls and women in our culture. There would be backlash to my truth, my suffering, my pain, and my voice. Critics would rise high above to tear me to pieces in hopes that I would fall, bury myself in shame, and be silent once again, this time forever. I would be called names and given numerous, unpleasant titles. My physical form would be degraded and criticized. Every action I took in life would never be good enough. I would be shredded to pieces.

I know all of this must've scared you, too.

Was this something I could handle? Would I be able to stand being raped again? First by the Kuta, then by the justice system, and then by the public for speaking my truth? Would I be able to survive it? How would I protect myself? How would I protect my daughters? My family? There was so much to think about. Why would I want to stand naked in front of the whole world on a big screen worldwide? Wasn't standing naked in court enough? Why would I want to be shredded to pieces by anyone else? Why would I want to take on another fight? A battle more brutal than the court case? A battle that would follow me to my deathbed? A battle that might not bring about the change that I so desperately wanted for my girls, family, and others?

The answer to all the questions that popped up in my mind was simple: *I must.* Encrypted in every cell of my body were those two words: *I must.*

I must protect my daughters.
I must stand up for Little Jeeti and my sisters.
I must rise to stop the vicious cycle of sexual abuse in my family and culture.
I must not let fear stop me.
I must be true to myself.
I must speak my truth.

I couldn't have stopped if I wanted to. I was ready and prepared to face whatever came my way. I would stand in my truth and the inner personal power that comes from it. I was willing to risk it all.

You see, honey, there are things in life worth standing up for no matter what the consequences may be. Ever since life began for me, I was put in a large arena, much like the old Roman coliseum, filled to its maximum capacity with spectators seated all around me. There were so many faces in the crowd, some I recognized clearly while others were only a blur. I saw the faces of my parents, uncles, aunts, cousins, and extended family members. I saw Pago, Parmar, Papa, Priest, and all the other men that touched me inappropriately. I saw the Kuta and the women and men that protected him. I saw children from my school, teachers, neighbours, members of my community, both male and female, young and old. They were all there to throw stones. Some hit me hard and crushed my body while others left bumps and bruises. But together, they worked to crush, kill, and participate in the silent stoning of Little Jeeti.

I did not want our daughters to suffer the same fate as me. I did not want our daughters to be silently stoned. I did not want this to continue happening to Little Jeeti, my sisters, and other little girls, children, and women across the world. That's why I knew, no matter what, that *I must* help bring change into this world. *I must* do my part in making this world a better place for our daughters, little girls, and women. *I must* flush the Kuta out of the shadows. *I must* shine light on the sexual abuse in our brown culture.

And *I must* keep faith you will be by my side.

Have you ever considered, my love, that perhaps you came into this world to be a companion on this journey? To be a husband to a courageous woman like me? Has the thought occurred to you that perhaps you are in my life as a soul who is here to walk alongside so I can heal? For us both to heal together and protect our daughters and our future generations from the cycle of abuse? Have you also considered that instead of having financial wealth and material riches, our true wealth can be found in my healthy emotional and physical health and that of our daughters? Do you know that you have helped empower me to raise girls who will go on to raise and empower their own sons and daughters?

I get this is not the life you signed up for when we married, but do you realize the impact you've had on this earth by offering whatever support you could to a passionate person like me? Do you understand the impact on the girls, women, boys in our culture? You have had a huge hand in the ripple effect of me breaking my silence. You have been an essential part of the ripples flowing through our family system and culture. Without knowing it, you have set an example for other males to be supportive of their wives who have suffered similar stories.

My love, I get I'm not the wife you expected. I know the journey I have embarked on is long and arduous. I know you may tire along the way when you're by my side. If you need to sit and rest, by all means do. If you tire and feel this path is not one for you, I will understand. If you, along the way, decide to choose a path that leads away from the footsteps I have left behind, I will love you regardless. No matter what, I will never be able to express what your love and you standing beside me has meant.

You will always be my Sohna.

I will love you forever.

With Love,

Your Precious
Beloved
Jeeti

LETTER 19

You Were Right All Along

Dear Dr. Alexander Lees,

It wasn't until November of 2016 that I was finally able to testify against the Kuta. You had already passed away, going into soul land earlier that year. I had been seeking your help off and on for ten years at that point. You knew me better than I knew myself then.

You always used to say, "People are not broken and in need of fixing. Most people are just fine. They simply need a tune-up." I trusted you and valued you as a mentor. You were way ahead of your time, using different modalities and unconventional methods of therapy to help your clients heal. You completely got the mind and body connection and the ability us humans had to rewire our brains. You had so much knowledge and wisdom to share, and I loved learning every bit I could from you.

I completed your EFT certification workshops and became certified as an EFT practitioner myself. You understood the power of energy psychology, and you helped me find my own inner power. I remember your eyes lighting up when you introduced me to the real healing guru: myself!!

"The real healing guru is you," you said.

You loved using humour in therapy sessions. Many times I laughed, though other times I must confess I didn't get your jokes. You loved it when I would have my "Ah-ha!" moments. You loved when something would finally land with me. You saw my potential and magnificence. You saw something much more in me than I could see in myself at that time. You knew without a doubt I would be a leader who inspired others one day.

Dr. Lees, you won't believe how I sat in the court witness box for an entire week, sharing traumatic details of my past and being grilled by a defence that repeatedly painted me as a liar with an ulterior motive. I was put on the defensive and treated as if I was the one who had committed a crime. Every detail of my sexual history before and after I was 11 years old was explored as well. In all of it, it was the breathing, tapping, timeline therapy, and the other techniques you taught me that helped me get through it. I even used some of these techniques to help my sisters cope with the whirlwind of emotions, anguish, and trauma we found in court. You would have been so proud to see me apply your teachings.

Salakshana and Kira testified the following year in Williams Lake. The witnesses for the defence and even the Kuta himself testified later that year, too. Through all the years, the trial moved at a snail's pace, courtesy of tactics used by the defence to cause delay, delay, and more delay. One time, it was a calculated last minute request to ask for our counselling records. Another time, it was offering to change his plea to guilty. One time, it was changing lawyers. Yet another time, he had an issue with the Punjabi transcripts. One time, he was claiming he had run out of money to fund his defence. And another time, it was that he couldn't appear because of illness. Excuse, after excuse, after excuse. For some reason, the judge kept on granting the defence adjournment after adjournment, seemingly incapable of taking charge of his own courtroom. It seemed time was not of the essence to anyone but us—the ones that had been victimized.

No one cared about the trauma and turmoil being inflicted

upon me and my sisters. The rescheduling of new court dates far into the future, the rereading of police statements, the packing and unpacking of suitcases, the time spent away from family, the reliving of our deepest traumas—it all took a toll on my sisters and I. I watched my sisters wither away in emotional turmoil and suffer in physical health. My daughters and niece were also affected in ways yet to be realized. I too was tired and stressed. What started out as standing up for the truth had become a bigger cause—a cause that would help other survivors coming through the system. That's why I had to keep going.

I wished you were alive, Dr. Lees. I had moments where I would go from feeling like shit, losing faith, and giving up hope back to optimism, enthusiasm, and keeping faith that this would be finished once and for all. There was a silent power within me that kept me bouncing back, fueled up and ready to face the next hurdle. Drawing on this power and using the self-help tools you taught me, I kept myself together, remained confident, and continued doing whatever I could to help the case along. I attended almost every hearing, wrote letters to officials in hopes of finding someone to do something about the unnecessary defence delays, and helped the Crown prosecutor with whatever information she needed.

Our Crown prosecutor, Ms. Julie Dufour and RCMP Victim Services support worker, Mick Howell were amazing. It was as if the Universe had sent angels to walk beside me and my sisters through what it knew would be a long brutal journey. Mick was very grounded, nurturing, kind, compassionate and offered us the brotherly and father like male support that me and my sisters needed. Ms. Dufour was passionate about her work, attentive, loving, full of compassion and empathy, and one of the smartest women I'd ever met. She listened to what I had to say, gave me the time and attention I needed to understand the proceedings, and was there for me when I was angry and tempted to give up hope. She was someone I could trust with my life. With Ms. Dufour by our side, we were in such good hands. She went above and beyond to understand the case, my sisters, the evidence, my culture, and the many nuances that impacted the details of our lives. She worked tirelessly long hours into the late night over the years and did her best to move the case forward. She was my rock through the case. She connected with me in such a high level of trust and honesty, it left me feeling heard, seen, safe, nurtured, and with the knowingness that I would be okay no matter what. I would not have gotten through the journey of our court case without her.

Finally, Dr. Lees, 11 years after our police report, the verdict was finally announced on April 6, 2018.

Guilty.

There it was: guilty on four out of six counts. For reasons incomprehensible to me, the judge found the Kuta not guilty for two sexual assault charges pertaining to Kira. That I will never understand.

That day we sat quietly in the Williams Lake courthouse: me, Kira, Salakshana, Sohna, my daughters, Jesse, and my cousin Babbu. We were there along with the entire film crew, support workers, the Tribune local newspaper gals, and eager members from the Crown's office as the judge read out the verdict. The only person present for the Kuta was Parm. With the reading, the courtroom burst out into cheers. Some of us were teary eyed. Despite the unfavourable outcome regarding her, Kira whistled in victory. We went outside immediately and danced to the loud drumming of Babbu on the dhol as the film camera rolled. They caught every part of this monumental, historical moment for four brown women: the three Pooni sisters and our cousin Babbu. We broke our silence, pursued justice, and got a conviction.

I felt elated. There was an electrifying energy inside and all around me. I felt the great-grandmothers and great ancestors dancing with us—their voices echoed with every drum beat, every footstep, every voice speaking up and standing in truth. My body had a momentum of its own. We were witnessing a historical moment in our brown culture. A moment where four Indian women rose against all odds to break their silence and speak their truth. It was a monumental moment for all sexual abuse survivors.

At that moment, the filming of our documentary wrapped.

As we rejoiced after the judgment, the defence proceeded with filing yet another application: Section 11(b) Charter Application (a delay application commonly referred to as the "Jordan Application"). They were asking the court for a stay of proceedings, claiming the Kuta's right to be tried in a timely manner was breached (even though he was the one who had asked for all the adjournments).

Basically, it's another loophole used by those who commit crime to get off free even after a guilty verdict.

This journey, as I had hoped, was not done yet.

With Love,
Jeeti

LETTER 20

I Did It, Dad

Dear Dad,

You bought me my first bicycle when I was around six years old. It was royal blue with a white banana seat. It was on a sunny day on the front street of our house when you tried to teach me how to ride my bike. I was afraid to ride the bike. I was afraid I would fall off, but more so, I was afraid of you. Afraid that you would yell at me and be disappointed in me if I didn't get it right. Scared, I got on to the bike and used the street curb to push forward slowly. You held the back of my seat and told me to pedal. Afraid you would yell, I pedalled quickly as the handlebar wobbled. You let go of the back of my seat, and I did it! Dad, yes I did! I learned how to ride my bike in just a few minutes with you.

You also taught me that I had to have good grades, which is why I made the Honour Roll in high school numerous times. My report cards were always good because I wanted to prove to you I could do it. And again, I was afraid you would get mad if I didn't. I played numerous sports, and my basketball team did well, but I don't ever remember you ever praising me. You didn't save any of my report cards or clippings of me and my basketball team from the local newspaper. I noticed back then that you had a special file for Jesse in your filing cabinet with all of his report cards and newspaper clippings of his sports teams. I felt I wasn't good enough and you would always be disappointed in me. I would never measure up, Dad, to a son, no matter what I achieved.

My eyes and ears have seen and heard you say a lot over my lifetime, and sometimes, I wished I was dead instead of having to listen to the things you said. It was during the filming of my documentary, *Because We Are Girls*, that something you said left me shattered, upset, and angry. I couldn't believe the words that came out of your mouth, Dad. Kira, Salakshana, and I were at your house to film family "tea" time with you, Mom, and Jesse for my film. The entire National Film Board crew was there as well. I knew what needed to be discussed: the shame, blame, and lack of support we received from you and Mom over the years. I also wanted to touch on the lack of male support period in our culture—something pivotal to address for the film. And I also wanted to flush out your thoughts and feelings to see if anything had changed inside you since the day I broke my silence almost a decade before.

You and Mom sat on the white sofa at your house in your formal living room. Kira and Salakshana sat on the loveseat together and Jesse on the chair. I sat on a cushion on the floor at the end of the glass coffee table situated in the middle of all of us. You and Mom were to my left, Salakshana and Kira to my right, and Jesse across from me.

I wanted a moment of silence to myself before the conversation started. I knew what had to be said to start the conversation and what we would each have to hear. I turned my attention to my tea cup and watched the hot vapours from my chai rise in mysterious shapes and patterns as my thumb and pointer finger caressed the brim of my white cup. Round and round on the brim went my finger until it took a short rest on the handle. My long nails looked bold and beautiful, polished in a bright, strong, and vibrant red (reassuring me of my inner power and strength). My ring sparkled with its many gems—a ring Little Jeeti would have loved to wear while playing dress up. The hot steam from my cup danced as if it knew the camera was rolling, oblivious of the conversation to follow. It was imaginative and playful with its moves, and I smiled as I watched it. This chai was different; it was our first family tea. We siblings had never gone over for tea at our parents', so it would have been an exciting, new time for our family on any other occasion. But we knew why we'd come. We knew that no one was going to enjoy this tea because we knew the conversation that was coming.

I could sense the unease in you, Mom, my siblings, and even the entire film crew in the room. It was my job to start the conversation—to ensure everything that needed to come out would come out over tea. This wasn't just a conversation between my own parents and their children; it was a much-needed conversation between parents and children in our culture and around the world. This conversation would give voice to millions around the world. It would challenge ancient beliefs that silence women and little girls. This conversation was one not even my parents, grandmothers, great-grandmothers, and ancestors dared to have in their families. That's because in the homes, families, and communities in our culture, it was still taboo. This was a big moment for so many. I closed my eyes, breathed deeply, and set the intention that the conversation would flow exactly as it was meant to with love and ease. I trusted all that needed to come out would be said. I also knew once Kira started, there would be no stopping her.

And then, the conversation started.

I brought up the lack of support we received from our parents in regards to the Kuta stuff. The conversation rolled from there. Mom admitted she was trying to hide the issue and you, Dad, responded by saying, "When I initially suspected there seemed to be something wrong, how many times did I tell you to avoid sitting with him?"

In your mind, you had been supportive.

"How were you? What did you do? Tell me in what ways you

supported us," I demanded in reply.

Numerous times you expressed how pointless you felt this conversation was to our family. Again, something you have said to me before came out of your mouth.

"In the Punjabi culture, there is an appropriate way to sit in the family. You have a responsibility, too," you said. "You should've sat in this proper Punjabi manner in the family. You didn't. You also weren't wearing appropriate clothing."

The clothing you were referring to were things I wore in my early teen years. Sometimes, I would wear my jogging pants above my calves; it was the fashion trend at the time. You didn't like that. But Dad, let me remind you that I always wore pants. I wasn't allowed to wear skirts or shorts, remember? The only time I wore shorts was when I played on my high school sports teams and I had to wear the team uniform for games. Have you forgotten, Dad, once the Kuta came to Canada, you ordered us girls to change from our school pants into our salwar kameez, our traditional Punjabi clothes, at home? Should I have worn a burka instead?

"I didn't sit beside the Kuta," Kira said to you during the tea. "He raped me anyways."

Kira was in a Punjabi salwar kameez when he raped her, Dad. You were quiet when she said that. Why did you have nothing to say to that? Why were you quiet? You weren't making sense, Dad. What planet were you living on? How could you for even a moment think that your daughters were to blame for their choice of clothes or which trusted relative they sat beside in their own home? Why should we have to share responsibility in what the Kuta did to us?

Not once during this tea did you mention how cruel or criminal it was of the Kuta to rape and sexually abuse your daughters. Was that because you felt more empathy for him, Dad? As a male, did you feel more loyalty to him—a criminal facing jail time? Was it easier for you to sleep at night by thinking your daughters must have done something wrong in order to be raped? Was it easier for you to swallow the fact that your daughters were raped by your nephew because of their clothing? We were children, Dad. How many times must I remind you of that? Not even wearing a burka would have stopped your nephew from raping your daughters.

"Why didn't you tell me back then?" you questioned us.

"I was only 11 years old!" I cried. "I didn't even know what he was doing to me. What was I supposed to tell you?"

I didn't have the language to put into words what the Kuta was doing then. I didn't have the mental capacity to understand what he was doing. I wasn't taught anything about my body, sex, or boundaries. I didn't know I was even allowed to have a boundary! Was I somehow magically supposed to know what was going on? I wasn't given a handbook about this stuff, Dad.

"Why do you keep forgetting I was a little girl, Dad?" I asked.

You had drilled so much fear inside us girls, Dad, rendering me powerless to say anything. You always punished us for the smallest things as children. Imagine how severe my punishment would've been for being raped and losing my virginity! You would have shipped me away to India and left me for dead. Well, Dad, you knew now. You had known for years by this point. What had you done about it since? You didn't even have a talk with the Kuta or a sit down like you'd said. What was I supposed to expect?

"You think where you have gotten and everything you have done, you did it all by yourself?" you asked me in anger.

Yes, Dad, I did. Who else do you think did it all? You? Mom? Uncle? Massi? Jesse? My sisters? As you, Mom, and the other adults sat in silence, I got to work. It was I that attended to my own mental, emotional, and physical health. It was I who attended to the immediate needs of my girls, husband, and myself. It was I who made sure my sisters were okay. It was I who consoled the Little Jeeti inside me and cried with her in her pain. I had to pick up the pieces on my own. I had to stand up and support myself if I wanted to protect my daughters, myself, and others. I had to stop that criminal and hold him accountable.

And the whole time, Dad, you did not ask if I was okay. You did not reach out to ask if I needed your help. You did not check to see if my marriage was okay. What would've happened to me and Maheema if Sohna had left? You did not call to see if I was dead or alive. You did nothing to hold the Kuta accountable. Instead, you blamed me because I was the one who was sitting beside him when I was younger. The one and only thing I hoped you would have done was sit him down and confront him, whether or not other family members supported you. But Dad, you didn't even follow through with that.

I had to do it myself, Dad. Why was that hard for you to swallow? Was it because I'm a girl? Was it unfathomable for you that I could actually do all this being a girl? Was it because I did more than you? Was it because I was able to look at shame right in the eye, be so vulnerable, and risk it all? Why was it so hard for you to accept my strength, Dad? Was it because I flexed my own muscles while you and the males around me chose not to flex yours? Did that make you feel weak? Did my courage and confidence scare you? Did it make you feel uncomfortable or even threatened? Would you have felt more comfortable if I had remained submissive, powerless, and broken? Was that why you didn't greet, hug, or look me in the eye every time I came to your house? Could it be your own shame, guilt, and feelings of failure as a father? Or is it because you would have to look at how you have treated women in your life and your attitudes and views about girls and women? I question if it's the shame and honour that kept your head bowed, rendering you powerless. Do you have a story, Dad?

Choose your words wisely, Dad. They have a way of coming back to bite you.

You always hugged Jesse and inquired about his well being every time he walked into the house. You looked him in the eye and would say "Here comes my future." Even Mom referred to him as her *"eik aunkh,"* meaning he was her one and only eye. Salakshana was so right when she said to you and Mom during the filming, "When Jesse walks into the house, it's as if God has walked through the doors."

It was no secret that your life and happiness revolved around him, your son. It was also no secret us girls, Salakshana, Kira, and I, were a bi-product of your quest and desire to have that son.

Jesse didn't get it either. He saw Kira and I sincerely seeking answers and questioning you as an attack. How could he ever possibly get it? How could he know what it was like to have a cold shoulder and an averted look from your own father? He had no idea what it meant to live as a girl child and be treated differently. He said I should hug you—that I should keep on hugging you until one day, you would greet me the same as everyone else. I disagreed, of course. I didn't think I should have to repeatedly prove myself to you and beg for your love, empathy, or support. Those things are supposed to radiate naturally from a father's heart.

You don't know, Dad, how hard and traumatizing it was for me to live my life as a raped Indian girl. You don't know the strength and courage it took me to break my silence and tell you I was raped by your nephew.

"It's like being in the middle of an angry, dark ocean that is drowning you wave after wave," Kira explained during the tea filming. "I reached out my hand for you and Mom to grab as I was being pulled downward by the turbulent water into the depths of the sea. You and Mom did not grab my hand. I was so desperately hoping you would. You did not pull me out and hug me, hold me, and tell me that you would protect me. You didn't say I was safe, that you were here for me, that you would believe and support me. Instead, you placed your hand on my head and pushed me deeper into the water to drown."

Her words speak for me and Salakshana, too.

Kira cried during the filming of our tea time that day. You were sitting right there, but you did not move to console her. I hugged her as she wailed in pain and anguish. Sitting right there in silence, you missed out, Dad. You missed out on the tight embrace of your little girl's arms clinging on to your shoulders for reassurance and the feeling of safety she desperately needed from her father. You missed out on comforting her as the old pain and trauma crawled up her body. You missed tuning into the Little Kira that was crying for help—crying to free herself from the pain and trauma the Kuta had inflicted. You missed the opportunity to help her feel safe in your arms. You missed the moment to correct a wrong inflicted upon her under your watch a long time ago. A simple hug would have done so much for her in that moment, but you missed it, Dad.

"I am here for you, child," I whispered over her in your place as I caressed her head. "You are safe. You are protected. You are loved."

She clung to me even more. Her soul held on to mine, and my soul consoled hers as I soothed her. Her heart heard the rhythm of mine and began to slow down. Finally, our hearts beat together in unison. She felt the love and strength of my tight arms around her and the power it transmitted into her body—powerful enough to punch out the Kuta wherever he still resided inside her. She started calming down, coming back to herself. And the whole time, you missed it, Dad.

You kept missing it, too. You never asked me about the court case. You never cared much about the documentary. Your remarkable Jeeti did something incredible. I created a documentary film to share the stories of me and my sisters. That film, *Because We Are Girls*, screened on May 1, 2019, a year after the verdict was announced. Dad, that film has rocked the world. It had its premiere in Toronto at Hot Docs International Film Festival, screening at prestigious venues including the Tiff Bell Lightbox and the grand Vancouver PlayHouse for the DOXA Documentary Film Festival. You did come to the sold out Vancouver premiere and saw the 675 person audience there to see it. You saw how moved they were, how much love they showered your daughters with, and how grateful they were that someone had the courage to finally wake up and bring to light the sexual abuse in our culture. It was long overdue, Dad, ripping the carpet off of this taboo topic and exposing the ugly truth.

The film sold out screening after screening. It lit audiences on fire, giving them a voice that finally allowed unthinkable conversations to be had amongst siblings, parents, friends, and families in our culture and other cultures, too. The year flew by as Kira, Salakshana, Baljit, and I went across Canada from one screening to the next. We took part in panel discussions, meeting the lineup of audience members and countless other souls who saw their stories being represented in our courage and vulnerability. They were able to relate to the film in such a magnificent, powerful way. They were real live people from various cultures who suffered in silence. Weighed down by the trauma from sexual abuse, they were able to acknowledge their own painful stories for the first time because of our film, knowing they were not alone. The media attention our story received from local and national media was unbelievable. Even the Indian media talked about the documentary and the court case. *The Williams Lake Tribune*, the newspaper Salakshana and I delivered door to door for a short period when we were little, picked up the story, too. Your daughters became known as the Pooni Sisters. We even have our own hashtag: #PooniSisters.

Your family name will be remembered forever, Dad. We have done our lineage proud. By breaking our silence in such a big, bold way, your daughters have started a revolution—an awakening in our brown community. We were being hailed as "*Shernis*" (lionesses), the flag bearers of justice, the heroes and revolutionaries of our community, the ones who have fallen on the sword to waken the community like Bhagat Singh.

You might think I'm making all this up in my head, Dad. Maybe you think my ego is wild with fame and narcissism. Come look at my inbox, Dad. It's lit up every day with messages from people of all ages, genders, backgrounds, and cultures. You have no idea how many messages I receive daily from others who have suffered rape and sexual abuse. It seems to have touched every home in some shape or form. And Dad, it may surprise you to know that even males are sharing their experiences with me! No gender is spared from abuse.

What's happening is so profound. It's an honour to bear witness to the ripples. The stories that followers are sharing with us are gut wrenching. There's so much grief, trauma, and sadness. Breaking my silence allowed these people to do the same. Of course, I'm no hero, Dad. There are others putting out good work in the world. There are others who have gone through much more intense suffering than I did. I am only a person who disobeyed and revolted against the suppressive forces of her culture and instead, followed her inner wisdom and broke her silence. I am a girl who stood up for herself, her sisters, and her daughters. I followed my desire to make the documentary come to life no matter what, and I'm so glad I listened to that inner voice, the knowingness, that told me to keep going. It did take a lot of hard work and required tremendous effort on my part. It also added extra stress on top of the court case journey for me and my sisters. The seva *(selfless service)* came right from our hearts with no financial payment in return. The documentary is a gift to our community, and the impact of the film has been immeasurable and worth the added stress.

How do you feel, Dad, knowing your daughters are referred to as revolutionaries? Perhaps now you can put up a picture of us three—me, Kira, and Salakshana—on your dining room wall as you had of our cultural icons, revolutionaries Bhagat Singh, Raj Guru, and Sukhdev, when I was younger. This film has been a gift to our future generations, our community, to the world. It's a gift I hope you can be proud of, too.

Soon after the release of the documentary and more than a year after the guilty verdict, the judge's decision on the delay application the Kuta had filed came in. The judge granted the Kuta the application, and the case was stayed. What this meant, Dad, was that the Kuta was still guilty in the eyes of the Canadian justice system and the conviction would stand, but he would not be sentenced to any jail time. Now, all charges against him were dropped. He would have no criminal record, and he was not required to register on the sex offender's registry list.

Upon hearing the awful decision, I asked myself what I should do next. To me, it was obvious: When all systems fail, go straight to the top. I immediately got to work, making a social media video addressing Prime Minister Justin Trudeau and other policy makers. I officially wrote to them as well. I set up a petition for the #PooniSisters on Change.org to gain public support and ensure the Crown would appeal the decision. The petition garnered over 60,000 signatures. The court's decision to stay the case brought more media attention to the case and more media interviews for me. And eventually, it paid off. The Crown did decide to appeal the decision on the stay of charges. I don't know how much of what I did had to do with this turn of events. I will never know, and that's okay. The only thing I know for sure is that I did not give up. I never strayed from my truth.

The appeal was heard in the British Columbia Court of Appeal by five judges, including the Chief Justice Baumann himself. It's rare for five judges to be appointed, Dad; it's usually only three. This was a very important case, and depending on how the judges ruled on this appeal, the case could go back to the Supreme Court of British Columbia for sentencing or further on to the Supreme Court of Canada. The case could make new case law that would affect other cases like it. So, we waited patiently for the decision to be announced the following year.

As you know, the year 2020 brought more change than any of us expected. We hit the international festival run in the spring with the film, receiving more national and international media coverage. Our first UK premier was in Scotland, and then we were supposed to go to London, Los Angeles, San Francisco, and elsewhere. It was so exciting, but my excitement was short-lived. Covid shut down everything after Glasgow. All plans to travel and meet audiences worldwide were halted. The shutdown was the onset of other shutdowns to come. It was the beginning of so much more than we realized.

During that year, I wrestled with the part of me that was feeling done with the whole criminal court case journey. It had been year, after year, after year of trauma and drama in the courts. I wanted to move on. I didn't know how much more we could take. There was the possibility the matter could drag on for years to come depending on the BC Court of Appeal decision. The decision came in on February 10, 2021. All five judges dismissed the appeal and upheld the previous stay of case decision.

This was not the answer we hoped for.

This decision brought an end to the lengthy court case saga. It was made clear to me that the Crown would not appeal the case to the Supreme Court of Canada despite my next round of official letter writing to government officials. A part of me was upset, angry, and disappointed, and the other part of me was accepting of the fact that the criminal justice system nightmare was finally over. I could let go. I had done my best, and now it was time for me to move on. My sisters and I had sounded the alarm bells about the Kuta. We had done our due diligence. We had done more than our share over those 14 years.

I have so much good work to do, Dad, and this was the Universe's way of making sure I would not expend another ounce of energy in the court case saga. That journey had served its purpose in my growth, and now it was time for me to create and bring to life my big, bold vision that graced my vision board. Now, I could focus on fulfilling my purpose. I really meant it when I said to you years earlier in Punjabi, "I'm not born to do small things."

But before we close, I need you to know this, Dad: Though we are all grown up now, the little girls that were violated and tortured by the Kuta still live within your daughters. They still want to be loved and nurtured by their father. The Little Kira, Little Salakshana, and Little Jeeti will always live within us, and I am doing my best to give them the love and empathy they deserve. I am doing my best to fill your void, Dad, and nurture these little girls and their souls.

I am doing the job I wish you would do.

With Love,

Jeeti

LETTER 21

Strength Is a Muscle

Dear Mom,

As a young girl, I witnessed it all.

Like schoolyard bullies, both Dad and Uncle would ridicule you and purposely piss you off. I hated it when they made fun of you. It made me feel angry and sad. You did stand up for yourself and fight back. I was around six years old when you locked them out of the house late at night to make your point. I didn't know exactly what was going on, but I knew that whatever was happening, I was on your side. I saw your strength, determination, and power.

As a mature woman, I saw you stand up to Papa (your own father) to challenge his authority as he tried to bulldoze you over. You put him in his place so he couldn't exercise unnecessary authority over you. You let him know you were the boss soon after he landed from India. This was your house and your rules. Over the years I watched you change and become stronger. There existed only two women in my world back then who I believed could kick men in the butt: you and Wonder Woman. And I loved you both.

You were 26 when you came to Canada. You never wore makeup, thinking it was inappropriate culturally for a woman who had birthed four children to do so. You had three living daughters, and between me and Salakshana, you also had a son.

"His name was Umba," you would tell us. "He was tall, fair, and plump."

Umba fell ill when he was three days old and died when he was only nine days old. You often shared conflicting stories with us about his death. Once, you said the midwife did not boil the scissors before cutting the umbilical cord so he died of tetanus. With tears rolling down your cheeks during another painful story, you told us it was "jadoo toona," meaning, *"black magic."* You would say that because you bore the first Pooni son, he was poisoned.

Culturally, having so many children at such a young age classified you as old. Plus, you were married into a family whose elders were Kuka Sikh's. They were very simple and wore only white clothing. You came from India with only Indian clothes, three pairs of colourful sulwaar kameez, two saris, and one pair of embroidered leather khussa *(traditional embroidered handmade Punjabi shoes).* Dad ordered you a three-piece set ensemble from the Sears catalogue that came with a pair of stretch pants, a blouse, and a skirt. You never would wear that skirt. You were too shy and had never shaved your legs.

I remember how excited you were when you got your first job. It was a job as a dishwasher washing dishes by hand for $2.00 an hour. You went to work in your shinny khussa, your only pair of nice shoes, even though they slipped on the wet floor of your work. You washed each and every dish there by hand. I remember how hard you worked, the late hours you put in, and the gash on your thumb when you cut your hand on a broken plate at work. You wrapped up your thumb and continued to work, ignoring your injury. Your boss liked you because you worked fast.

Remember your very first car and how hard you fought to get it? Dad wouldn't buy it for you, and you were so upset. You walked a couple of miles each way to and from work, often walking home late in the dark on the highway. One day a police man stopped and asked if you needed a ride. You politely declined. From then on, you would put a jacket on your head as you walked home alone in the darkness so people wouldn't know you were a woman. Otherwise, you risked beer bottles being thrown at you by the racists in the community.... or worse.

Soon, you got your $500 car: a small, gray four-door car. I was so happy for you. I loved sitting in your car. Uncle called it your "bakki," referring to it as a horse. For a woman who wasn't allowed to ride a bike in India, driving and owning a car was so empowering for you. It was empowering for me to see you drive, Mom. Not very many Indian women drove back then. Even fewer had a driver's license or their own car. You really were the boss! If only you knew how my heart lit up and burst with joy every time I saw your car coming down the hill and into the garage. You came home faster in your car, and you had no idea how Salakshana, Kira, and I longed for you to come home from work. We would watch the hill and keep count of every car that drove by before you came home, wishing it was you. It made time go by a little faster and the wait for you more bearable. Other times we would fall asleep in front of the TV waiting up for you. We yearned for you, Mom. We missed you and craved your attention. We loved, respected, and adored you. You were our shining light.

I watched everything you did, Mom. I watched how you ran the household, how you handled responsibilities, how you tackled the good times and the bad times, and how you used your voice to shake the walls of the entire house if you had to. I watched you be the strength of our family. You encouraged Dad to help immigrate one relative from India after another so you could fulfill your obligations to your extended family. It was hard for you to watch your siblings and cousins suffer back home. You were expected to share your good fortune with them; that's what being a family is all about, right? You opened your home to each and every one of our family members. You financially helped them settle here, too. You took on a mother-figure role, tackling so much stress for all these people. You did not rest until they were all settled. I don't know how you kept your sanity in all the chaos. I wish my sisters and I had you all to ourselves so we wouldn't have been neglected and lost in the chaos. Our house was like a revolving door of immigrant relatives coming and going constantly over the years. You were so brave and strong. Where would all these people be without you?

Growing up, you were my role model. I admired your strength and courage. I wanted to be strong just like you. I learned so much about resilience and strength from you, Mom. I thought you were God. Even though you didn't get a full education or know how to speak very much English, you commanded yourself as if you had a PhD. You were a born leader. I drew from your strength, Mom. There was no task you couldn't do. You were creative and always found your way around challenges.

Guess what, Mom? I grew up to do the same! I began to challenge males and authority figures just like you did. I learned to stand up for myself. With every crack that Dad, Uncle, Masser, my other uncles, and the Kuta took at me, I did not back down or wither away. Instead, I became stronger and stronger. Facing and enduring every put down and attempt to smother my voice by those who claimed to love me, I got stronger. So strong that ultimately, I found my self worth, my value, and my voice. I found the courage to speak my truth and hold the Kuta accountable—a feat no one else dared to accept.

I became so strong and resilient that not even a long, drawn-out journey through the criminal justice system in holding the Kuta accountable could take me down. From the very first day I broke my silence about being raped by the Kuta until now, my inner strength has grown beyond my expectations. The more I draw on my own inner power to overcome each challenge, the stronger I become. Now, I feel like Wonder Woman. I feel just like you. Each day I look at my girls and remind myself to stand tall, strong, and confident, like a mighty oak tree so grounded and deeply rooted into Mother Earth that nothing can shake me. I stand tall and strong, like I remember you standing, Mom.

But there is one thing I have done differently than you, Mom. It's the one thing that has allowed me to tap into the strength of Wonder Woman and Hercules combined. I have chosen to face the truth of my past and not hide from it. I've chosen to deal with the ugly truth of all the sexual abuse by Pago, Parmar, Papa, Priest, and the Kuta. I want the same for you, Mom. I yearn for the day to come when you face the truth of all that has happened to you as a woman. I hope you find a way to embrace it no matter what it is. To stop running away from it and not keep it stuffed inside. To stop with the lies and trying to quiet the voices of your daughters. To stop lying to yourself.

Those things keep you from getting to know the real you. They keep you in hiding in a restless, dis-eased state of self disgust and shame. I'm not saying you have to relive your traumatic past, bringing up each and every horrific memory and announcing it to the whole world. What I'm saying is that I hope you can acknowledge your own story and your own wounds to yourself. That you can honour yourself and your true essence. That you can finally let whatever has been sitting deep inside you, suppressed for centuries, out. You don't have to share it with anyone else, Mom. You can share it with the trees when you are out on a morning walk or the flowers that you plant and love every spring season.

I know you were once an innocent little girl, too. I can't imagine how hard life must have been for you then. I often wonder what kind of a life you had as a child. What coping mechanisms did you adopt for survival? What did you do to have your basic needs met? I often wonder if, as a girl born in India, you ever received the love and nurturing you deserved. Who wiped away your tears when you cried? Who hugged you the times you needed to be held and soothed? Who was there to take away your sorrow, shower you with unconditional love, and heal your pain? You were forced to swallow your own tears and wipe them away quietly so no one would see. You had to hug yourself to sleep. You were forced to keep your difficulties to yourself, bury your pain and trauma, and snuggle into the blanket of shame and silence every night.

You often said that living life in India was very difficult for you. You told stories of your childhood where your mother bought you red glass bangles from a pilgrimage you two had embarked on when you were around nine years old. When you came back home, Papa was enraged and ordered your little brother to smash them with a rock while you were wearing them. Of course, you cried. You weren't allowed to wear bangles. You, your mother, and your siblings weren't allowed to dance or sing. You couldn't attend local weddings in your village. Papa was very strict. Papa was always away following his communist ideology and helping others by doing social work in nearby villages. He didn't pay much attention to feeding his own family. It was his mother, your grandma who looked after the daily household matters. As a child, you slept with your grandma and called her Bēbē (*pronounced Bay-bay*). You used to tie a drawstring to your ankle and the other end to hers so she wouldn't leave you alone in the bed at night. Your mother died when you were 19 years old. How much you wished it was the other way around—your father being dead instead.

I remember you crying once and saying a Punjabi saying: *"When I step inside my home, it's the mice that would eat at me, and when I step outside, it's the crows that would eat at me."* You were referring to the men inside your own family and the men outside in your extended family, village, and community in India. You also said something that still gives me the shivers today: *"In India, men don't even leave the alley female dog alone. What is a woman to them?"*

It must have been hard for you to protect yourself from men—men preying on little girls and women because they knew they'd get away with it. They knew they had the ultimate weapon on their side: the power of shame, blame, and family honour. Women had to bow to the power of shame; they had to force little girls to bow, too. They all had to keep silent for survival, accepting sexual abuse as something that normally happens and carrying on with their lives as if nothing happened. They had to keep their stories and secrets of a culture buried, allowing the cycle of abuse to continue. That's why you normalized it too, Mom, and told Salakshana when she was younger that this is something that happens to girls and women.

I can't imagine what it must've been like for you to have a father like Papa—a father who preyed on children. I will never forget what he asked me to do when I was little, and I will never forget what one of your sisters said that Papa had asked her to do when she was a young girl. He wanted her to touch his penis and slide it in her hand back and forth. She told Bēbē when she was little, and Bēbē told her then to try and avoid being alone with him. I remember you were upset at your sister for sharing this story. I can't imagine what you might have suffered at the hands of Papa and other males growing up, Mom. You perhaps have a story more horrific than mine. You may have had to endure far more pain, trauma, and suffering than any of your daughters. To date, you have never told your daughters anything about rape or sexual abuse. You act as if the Universe had magically spared you. Yes, what a gift it would be if you were spared. But if the colourful platter of life presented so much rape and sexual violence in my life, I can only imagine the type of hues and experiences that were presented on your platter. I can only imagine what my grandmothers, great-grandmothers, and their mothers have been through. I can only imagine the hell you all had to endure and the sacrifices you had to make in a culture dominated by men using women's bodies to quench their insatiable thirst. Men who took full advantage and hid behind the veil of shame adorned by women.

The silence and shame sewn through every fibre of your

being is bursting at its seams, Mom. It's begging to be released. It's time to be silent no more. It's okay to speak up. Let that little girl inside you speak, Mom. Let her break free so she feels like a Wonder Woman, too. Let her tell her story. Hear her story, Mom, and see her wounds. Only you can ensure she is heard and seen. Nurture her, Mom. Give her the love and attention she deserves—the unconditional love and attention she never got. Don't push her down and ignore her any longer. It's already been far too long. Let that little girl inside you break free from the prison of shame and silence. Let her scream and roar as she was meant to. Let her confront her abusers, be they dead or alive. Let her share her story with whomever she chooses, even if it's only with you. Let her find peace and healing.

Come, Mom.

Come breathe the fresh air of freedom from the other side.

Come hear the giggles of the little girl inside you and feel her innocence.

Come hear the laughter of your daughters and play with us in our pureness and innocence.

Come hear the powerful melody.

It's okay if you are afraid. It's okay if you tremble. Don't let fear hold you back. No matter what, no matter how horrific your past, whatever choices you had to make for your survival are all good. They have made you who you are, and I will always love you, Mom. I will be with you along your journey, I promise. I will be there through your heartache and tears as you reunite with the little girl inside you. I will be there as you look for the long lost treasure chest of self love, acceptance, worth, and innocence. They are your long lost precious jewels calling for you to be reclaimed. They are the jewels that will help you heal.

Don't betray the little girl, Mom. She has already been betrayed countless times in your lifetime and over centuries. You can stop blaming the little girl now, Mom. It's okay; I am here for you. We will hug and hold each other with the tenderness and love we so rightfully deserve. I will wipe away your tears as you wipe away mine.

Together, we will wash away the pain of the little girls inside of us both.

Together, we will move forward, day by day, to reclaim the innocence of that little girl inside each of us.

Together, we will help her gain her voice and find her divine light.

There is nothing that you have done wrong, Mom. You are not to carry the burden of blame or shame on your shoulders. Your shoulders are too small to carry the burden of thousands and thousands of years of abuse and oppression in our culture. It's time to stop the cycle of abuse so it does not get passed down to your grandchildren, Mom. It's time to break away from the narrow-minded, limiting beliefs of a culture that fastened these shackles on you. I have the key, Mom, and so do you. The power is in our hands.

Look at the impact of standing in my truth and breaking my silence in such a big way, Mom. I did it for myself, my daughters, my sisters and others like you. Just look how much further the ripple effects have travelled to sexual abuse survivors around the world. Their messages to me confirm the impact.

You have saved my life.
You have no idea how many lives you have impacted.
Your entire community is in your debt for all that you have endured and the work you continue to do...
Your courage is justice for all women and girls.
Thank you for your bravery and not giving up!

There is now a global tribe of wonderful souls that stand by your girls, Mom. And they will all stand by you, too.

Together, we will find healing and radiate in our strength to make this world a better place for your granddaughters, their daughters, and future generations. We will make this world a better place for all the little girls, women, and children.

Let me know when you are ready. It will be an honour to be by your side.

With Love,

Jeeti

LETTER 22

Wake Up, Brother

Dear Brother,

You walk the earth as a man, oblivious to what it is like to be born a girl. You say you get it, but I don't think you do. Your physical form walks taller and stronger, pumped with much more testosterone than mine. It dominates my shadow at every turn. You say I am granted equality. You say there are policies and systems in place to protect me. You tell me not to worry, for you have the mightiest and most lethal weapons known to mankind. You tell me there are politicians advocating for me and governments mightier than God who have my back. You say you have read writings from the sages, rishis, gurus, ancient scriptures from the followers of God, and even from God itself. You say it is in my best interest to be guided and protected by you no matter which country I reside.

I do not think you understand, Brother.

I am a girl child, who throughout history has been suffocated to death by the palm of a hand, blanket, or pillow. My tiny lungs have not been allowed to gulp the precious air you are entitled to breathe so freely and abundantly. I, as a girl child, have been killed millions of times with fingers that strap around my neck, leaving thumbprints on my tiny throat. In modern times, state-of-the-art equipment has been used to kill me before birth. My tiny arms and legs have been given no chance to grow, my heart no chance to pump, my brain no chance to develop and comprehend. I, Brother, am being killed in my mother's womb—the same womb whose rich nutrients and love you've been allowed to reap.

I want to live, Brother. I want to be given an equal opportunity to walk the earth, just like you.

You watch as the axe of inequality chops me to pieces. Every day you stand by as men hoot and holler at my curves and inflict cruelty upon me. Your silence protects the pedophiles and rapists. You say nothing to stop my gang rape. You stand silent as I am stripped naked in bazaars, burned alive, robbed of education, disfigured by acid, and forced to cover every inch of my body in a burka. You remain quiet as my genitals are brutally mutilated, invaded with foreign objects. You say nothing as my insides are pulled out. You stand there in complete silence as I am held as a sex slave in brothels around the world. You act as if you are in shackles—as if you are the one being victimized. You act as if these crimes are not your doing. I am not sorry to tell you this, but this is your doing. You are the patriarchy—the dominant masculine energy that emasculates itself and feeds off the glory of power by harming the most vulnerable.

I don't know what is better: to be raped over and over again or to be killed as a girl fetus and denied life forever. I have died a thousand deaths being raped and shamed in this lifetime. Either way, I am denied life, respect, worthiness, and love. Why can't I have it all? A life without rape, violence, abuse, and shame? Why can't I have the life you are granted so freely? Why do I have to give away my power to you, the man? Don't you know that I too have been given life by a power much greater than you? The same power that blessed you and granted your birthright has also bestowed the same on me. Who are you to rob me of life, Brother? I am your equal, whether you like it or not.

Every year I tie a Rakhri on you, Brother, giving you blessings for a prosperous, long, and joyful life. Every year you promise me protection. Where is your protection, Brother? Where is your promise? Where are you when I am raped, smothered, or killed? What good is Rakhri, Brother? What good is your promise of protection? What good are you to me and the rest of humanity?

It is you who inflicts these atrocities upon me by choosing to remain silent. It is you, Brother, who rapes me. I need no further proof. Your reaction to the Kuta and the likes of him says it all. You did not unleash your fury on the Kuta and knock him to the ground. You did not bash his face in with your mighty fist. You did not hold him by the neck and ask, "Who the hell are you to do this to my sisters? To those I love so dearly?" You did not make an example out of him by choking the life out of his penis so no man would ever think about raping little girls or women ever again.

You did nothing, remember?

And that nothing sent a clear message to all pedophiles and rapists. You say vigilante justice is barbaric. You have police forces and judicial systems worldwide to take care of the Kuta and his kind. I have knocked on that door too, Brother—the door of criminal legal justice. I was dragged through the system for 14 years only to be further traumatized and shamed.

You claim you are supportive, but you sit there in silence when your sister wails. You follow the lead of your role model: Dad. You carry the generational beliefs Dad has passed down to you, amplified by the cultural forces around you. The lens through which you see has become clouded, and your empathy gauge has malfunctioned as a result. You viewed the conversation with Mom and Dad during "tea time" as an attack on Dad. It was not an attack, Brother! Those were unspoken words—the feelings of daughters never conveyed to their father in this lifetime and through centuries of our lineage. They unveiled cries for help both Mom and Dad had failed to hear. Sadly, you did not hear them either, Brother.

You say that you gave us support. I say that support is not

ridicule, anger, and shaming displayed toward your sisters because you didn't know how to deal with the horror of rape in your family. Support is not a phone call or text message once in a blue moon. Support is being there from day one, right beside your sisters to let them know with conviction that you will protect them. Support is rising to take the lead as a man by telling Dad, "Let's go. If you aren't going to confront the rapist, I will." Support is letting the world know that no matter what, you will always love, believe, and stand by your sisters. Support is sitting in court from day one to send a clear message to the rapist that you believe your sisters. Support is what your sisters needed to hear and feel over and over again when we broke our silence, standing naked in front of the whole world draped in the shame of having been raped. Support like this is something we need from you still, Brother, in order to create safer homes and communities for our children. Homes and communities where no sister will ever be raped.

It is not too late. You still have time. There is only one way to prove me wrong, Brother. You must deconstruct the inequality that exists. I dare you to make me your equal. I dare you to ignite the flame and carry the torch that will light the spark of equality in the mindset of every brother and father on this planet. I dare you to bring true equality for little girls and let them shine in their divine feminine energy. I dare you to stand up to all those who call your sisters liars.

You do not need an army; it all starts with you. All you need is you. It only took one David to bring down Goliath, remember? I know the power is within you, Brother. I've seen you use it to stand up for so many others to bring change. I have seen how you can mobilize over 250+ million people to gather in one of the largest human protests known to mankind—the Farmers Protest in India to bring change. I believe you can do the same for me.

Come stand with me, Brother. I would love to have you by my side. Take my hand and help me fight for my right to be equal. Help me dispel rape and violence against little girls and boys and men and women. Hurry, before I am smothered, choked, killed in the womb, burned alive, buried, raped, or beheaded. Hurry before it happens to someone else.

I'm not against you, Brother. I'm with you and for you. All I want is for my girls and yours—our children, grandchildren, and future generations around the world—to be able to live to their fullest potential. All I want is for you to join me in creating a world full of love and safety for all.

I have and always will love you, Brother.

With Love,
Jeeti

LETTER 23

Woman a Woman's Enemy... Why?

Dear Bēbē,

Mom loves you very much.

She talks about you often and has shared many memories about your strength and the hardships you endured.

She tells us stories of how you became widowed at the young age of 24. Your husband, my great-grandfather, Bakshish Singh Chhokar, died in Canada around 1927, leaving you with a young son, Papa. Mom also shared how your husband's dad, my great-great-grandfather, Sher Singh Chhokar, died in Canada a little later too. You were left in India to raise Papa, living with your extended in-law family. You also helped raise Papa's entire family when he married. You were revered by Mom, my Massis and all those who knew you as a strong woman.

Bēbē, I have many feelings I have longed to express to you.

I have carried a lot of guilt over my lifetime. It was as if I was born bundled in a blanket of guilt since conception. I felt tremendous guilt for not being able to protect my sisters and for believing the Kuta's stories and excuses. I felt guilty for having left my young sisters, cousins, and niece when they were the most vulnerable around him. I felt guilty for falling into the Kuta's trap and not being able to protect myself and my virginity. The burden of guilt grew heavier and heavier with each passing day. The weight of guilt was just as heavy as the weight of shame. In fact, the guilt brought on more showers of shame. It was a vicious, never-ending cycle.

How could I have failed my sisters and the young girls in my family?
How could I have failed myself?
How could I have been so stupid? So blind? So naïve?

When the time came for me to break my silence, I rose up like a lioness harnessed with all my courage and strength to do whatever it took to tell my truth, stand up for Little Jeeti, and protect my daughters and other young girls in our family. I didn't muzzle my sisters. I didn't blame them like Mom had blamed me when she told Salakshana, "If Jeeti hadn't sat close to Manjit, my other daughters wouldn't have been abused." I didn't cry and use emotional blackmail. I didn't abandon them. I didn't try to stop them. Unlike my Mom, I would never guilt anyone into silence. The weight of my own guilt and the loads of shame were too much to bear; I would never want anyone else to carry the same.

I first started to chip away at the guilt and the shame I felt inside in Dr. Lees' office. There, I was able to understand the skillful crafting and grooming of Little Jeeti by the Kuta. He used such precision, skillful workmanship, and tools to build the world he wanted me in. It took many sessions with Dr. Lees to start the process of decoding and rewiring my brain. It took years to crawl out from under the programming, pain, and trauma the Kuta had inflicted on me, and there would be many more layers to peel away over time.

Bēbē, I often wonder what you must have felt when one of my Massis (your own granddaughter) told you about Papa, your only child. Did you ever talk to him about it? Did you try to hold him accountable? I know you told her to avoid being alone with him, but that wasn't enough. You put it on her, Bēbē. She was a little girl herself. Did you mean to silence her like my Mom silenced me and my sisters? Did you do anything to protect the rest of your granddaughters, including my Mom? You kept it all quiet, Bēbē, giving him more power in our family. You let him have the green light to harm others, including your great-granddaughter, Salakshana.

Well, he was sexually inappropriate with me, too, Bēbē. It happened years before my trip to India when I got to meet you and spend time with you. Did you say something to him before you died in your old age? Or did you leave this earth carrying the guilt and shame forever? Did the blazing burial flames communicate anything to you about the cycle of abuse? Did you finally see how it festered in the silence?

Mom followed your footsteps, Bēbē. Mom did not expose Papa or hold him accountable for sexual abuse. Instead, she allowed the cycle of abuse to continue down into our family. When I confronted Papa on his visit in 2009, Mom was not really part of the conversation. She did little more than try to protect herself and deny anything ever happened to her. She flailed her arms in the air as she yelled from the kitchen, "Mainu ni kuj vi hoya. Mainu ni kuj vi hoya," meaning, *"Nothing happened to me."* Kira and Salakshana were present, too. I had told my Dad and Jesse I was going to confront Papa. Dad chose to stay in his bedroom, and Jesse protected Papa by shaking his head and yelling at me.

"It's terrible what you are doing to this old man. You should be ashamed of yourself," my brother shouted at me.

All I wanted was for Papa to know I remembered what he had done, I wanted him to know it was wrong and traumatic. Salakshana and Kira got to say their piece too. Mom didn't kick Papa out. Dad didn't say anything to him either. Mom still served him for days until he finished his visit. Life had given her another chance to stand up to a pedophile, face her guilt, and do the right thing by standing alongside her daughters, but she could not do it. She failed once again, just like she had with the Kuta numerous times. She couldn't do anything about it. Instead, she followed in your footsteps, Bēbē, carrying more guilt in silence and quietly allowing Papa, the Kuta, and others like them to go free without taking any responsibility or accountability.

Why are women so vested in protecting men, Bēbē? Why do they do so at the expense of innocent children and their own demise? Do they not see that the men are having women do their dirty work? Why is it, Bēbē, that even women blame little girls and women when all the while they know what it's like to live a life as a girl child in this world?

Take for example all the women that stand by the Kuta. For instance, Parm, who wanted me to apologize for my part in being raped and sexually abused by her brother, the Kuta. She said I had to be held accountable if the Kuta was going to be held accountable. She and the Kuta's family concocted their own truth without asking me or any of my sisters what he had actually inflicted upon us. She only saw me as a consenting adult; she never tried to see the 11-year-old girl I once was. How could the women around him live with the guilt of knowing he harmed my sisters and cousin too? How could they continue being blind, putting other girls at risk? I'm sure they didn't sleep well over those 14 years worrying that their poor brother might go to jail.

What about the girls who are raped and sentenced to a lifetime of trauma, pain, and suffering? Does anyone ever worry about them, Bēbē? The feelings of shame, dirtiness, loneliness? The hell they live day in and day out? As women, we all suffer, but the suffering compounds when women relish in the suffering of other women. It grows when men in our culture stand in their glory watching the drama, victorious and silently rejoicing at being protected by women. They act as if rape and sexual abuse doesn't happen to boys and young men, but as you know, it happens to boys too, Bēbē.

As a 10-year-old girl, I remember seeing something in your

eyes during my trip to India. Behind the light, there was sadness, Bēbē. It was a sadness illuminated with guilt and smothered in shame. I saw it in the women who came to protect the Kuta in the courtroom. I see it in my Mom, and I'm sure I must have carried it, too. Oh, how the guilt weighs one down no matter how much we deny what's happening around us.

Why is the world full of women who suffocate their own kind and live as carcasses filled with shame and guilt, Bēbē? Why is it that we women protect the abusers, be they our sons, fathers, brothers, grandfathers, or husbands? Why do we let the horrific harm in our families and culture continue? Why is it that we as women perpetuate abuse that is inflicted on our children? Do we not see our role in this? Our hand in carrying the cycle of abuse forward? Do we not see we are cutting ourselves at our own two feet and setting our children up for a lifetime of pain and suffering? Why do we not ask ourselves, "Exactly who are we women protecting?" Why are we so blind and asleep? Why would we rather live in guilt and be so vested in protecting the males at the expense of our children? Guilt is no easy burden to carry. It poisons and erodes you. It's killing us and our children, Bēbē. What kind of mothers are we? The number of children committing suicide is horrendous. That's what we as a family and culture should be ashamed of!

Do you have any answers from the other side? Can you enlighten me? How can a woman point the finger of blame and shame at another when she too has usually experienced it herself? I've heard that 1 in 3 girls and 1 in 6 boys have experienced some sort of sexual abuse. That's 1.3 billion girls and women; yes, Bēbē, 1.3 billion who live in the world today. Even that figure I feel is too low a number. Sexual abuse is so under reported and kept tightly under wraps that there's no real way of knowing how many girls or boys have been abused in our world.

Oh, Bēbē, it grieves me. For centuries we women have been the ones who wash the bedsheets, make the beds, and fluff up the pillows in our homes. And we do it all knowing what happens to our daughters, sisters, and aunts on these beds. It is we women who allow rape and sexual abuse to fester in our culture, and it is we who must carry the ensuing guilt with us into eternity.

With Love,

Jeeti

PART FIVE

Healing

LETTER 24

Find Your Spiritual Path

Dear Maheema and Shia,

I must confess, breaking my silence and going through the criminal justice journey took a huge toll on me. I became old, wrinkled, and bloated with gray hair and knots in my shoulders the size of golf balls. I got a stiff neck, puffy face, and a fluttering in my ear that came and went as I waited adjournment after adjournment to testify and speak my truth in court. The stress was incredibly high. I felt so heavy and weighted. Kira said it was like being in a pressure cooker—the big green kind my Mom used to make dhal in with the jiggly thing on top of the tiny air vent. Stress hormones flooded my body every day. My cortisol levels were insanely high. I'm surprised I didn't suffer a heart attack from the amount of consistent stress my body was experiencing. Standing up for my truth was a painful, trying ordeal, but it was necessary for my healing. I needed it to find my voice and my place in this world.

Not in a million years would I have thought the thing that I had kept buried as a secret would be the very thing to open the doors of something sacred within me. Breaking my silence launched me on a journey into spirituality. It gave me an awareness of self. I didn't like it when others told me I was spiritual. I didn't even like it when Dr. Lees said it. I equated being spiritual with being religious, and that was one thing I was not. But as I dove into the work of healing and seeking justice, the pain and trauma I endured was nudging me to one day open the gates of an inner journey. It pushed me to walk on to the path that would lead me to join hands with my authentic self—the self I was born to be. It helped me see my true essence, my soul.

Prior to breaking my silence, the question I had asked myself many times was this: *What is my purpose in life? My passion?* The answer that came from inside was simple: a fashion designer. I was so creative and passionate about fashion that I thought I was going to be the world's greatest designer, joining the likes of Valentino, Galliano, Dolce & Gabbana, and Lagerfeld. My designs were immaculate with Bollywood influences encompassing western silhouettes. I thought I was born to create such luxurious designs with the richest and boldest fabrics, thereby making women feel confident and beautiful. I thought I was born to unite the luxurious rich textiles and the decadent designs of the east and the west, bringing Bollywood and Hollywood together in one wardrobe.

But Kudhoos (*Pumpkins*), making the choice to break my silence changed all that. It changed instantly the moment I hung up Parm's phone call. I didn't have to think twice. I didn't sway. I knew exactly what I had to do. It was at that very moment I unknowingly opened the golden gates of finding a connection with my inner self, a connection to the awareness that resides within: my spirituality. It was not obvious to me at the time. I was oblivious to the fact that making the choice to tell the truth was allowing me to realign with the Little Jeeti I was born to be. I was taking the first step to finding my true, authentic self.

As human beings, we all experience trauma and suffering in some way. No one gets a free pass. For some of us, it's rape and sexual abuse. For others it might be a battle with body image issues, a deadly disease, the loss of a job, the death of a loved one, a car accident, neglect or abandonment by a parent, or bullying. The possibilities of how suffering can come into our lives are endless. Each one of us has our own experience that is unique to us when it comes to trauma and suffering. My darlings, it is what you do with that endured suffering that really matters. How you choose to respond can either connect you to your inner essence or further disconnect you, causing more pain and suffering.

I truly feel what one has suffered has an underlying purpose. I knew I wasn't going to let my suffering go in vain. I knew I was going to stand up for Little Jeeti, my sisters, my daughters, and other girls the Kuta had hurt. I knew I would be a voice for all those little girls, women, and children in the world suffering from rape and sexual abuse. When I made that decision, it meant the 13 years of suffering under the Kuta in my younger years did have a greater purpose—a purpose I was waking up to.

Once I broke my silence, something profound started happening to me. The more I stood up for my sisters, Little Jeeti, and the other girls, the more I was realigning with my inner power and my true inner self—my soul. And the more I realigned with my soul, the stronger and more confident I became. Suddenly, everything I was doing felt right. The more I trusted in the guidance from my inner self, the less afraid I became of the unknown and what was to become of me. Consequences that had kept me quiet previously didn't matter anymore. I was walking into my purpose.

Prior to breaking my silence, I didn't know there was a powerful essence inside me. It was there through all the rapes and all the suffering. It was there consoling me and telling me to hang on and persevere. It was there during my deepest, darkest hour, when I was all alone in despair and chose to end my life. It was there watching me and never leaving as I remained unconscious for days. The difference between then and now was clear. I hadn't connected to it, acknowledged its existence, or tapped into its enormous power then.

Now, I know my power and the divine place it comes from.

Over the years as I waited adjournment after adjournment in the court case, I walked into the journey of discovering my spiritual self and my connection with the Universe. I started to go on walks around my beautiful neighbourhood. I started to ask myself: *Who am I? What am I? What am I doing here?* The questions swirled in my mind. I would listen to podcast after podcast from spiritual and self-help teachers to connect deeper with my soul and to dissipate the waves of frustration, fear, anger, and sadness. Sometimes the feelings were so overwhelming, I would have to tap myself as I walked and do the other processing exercises Dr. Lees had taught me. Sometimes I would cry as the dark, dense pain, anger, sadness, and fear lifted from my body. Other times I experienced mounds of joy and peace. I wanted to walk into the courtroom without the weight of fear and anger. My sweethearts, what started to happen on those walks changed me. Suddenly, I could see the trees and their every leaf, every blade of grass, every intricacy and beauty of the moss, the sky, the blooming roses and dahlia, birds, children at the school field, and other people out for a walk. It all connected me to my soul and moved the energy inside my body into a joyous, rhythmic dance. When the nonsense that played out in court would weigh me down, my walks and the connection to self I found in them livened my soul.

Every day on my walks, I watched and admired nature's wonderous essence all around me. I loved the vastness of the sky and how it reminded me of the vastness that existed inside of me. I was especially fond of the stillness of the trees. I was in awe of how peaceful they stood, how their branches swayed and how the leaves moved with the wind. No matter how hard it rained, how violently the wind blew, how many branches ripped off, or how the hot sun blazed on them, they stood tall and strong, taking every beating from Mother Nature. I was in complete awe of the trees and how they weathered it all. They stood in their power and glory no matter which storm came their way, and they reminded me of my life and what I had gone through. It was as if the trees were speaking to me, "Be strong, be tall, be confident, be deeply rooted, be grounded, be you." It was an amazing feeling. I felt the power of the trees. I felt I was an old grounded tree, a mighty Oak tree.

The rain never stopped me from my walks. Instead, it enabled me to experience something more powerful. The cold raindrops falling on my face sent sensational vibrations through my entire body. It was as if every drop was kissing my face and tickling the joy that resided inside me, making me smile and laugh out loud. It made my insides dance. Each drop, as it landed on my flesh, was sending a message to my inner self and vibrations to each and every cell of my body. It was silently communicating with my every cell—all 37+ trillion of them that vibrated back to communicate their joy, excitement, and gratitude. It raised my vibrations so I could radiate at a level where I could feel the power of the mighty Universe inside me, behind me, and all around me. Both the raindrops and my soul were reassuring me to keep following the path that I was on. If I did, then all would one day be well.

On one of my walks in early October 2017 (a year before the verdict), I experienced something very peculiar. I had listened to Oprah's "Super Soul Conversations" podcast with Deepak Chopra about the observer the day before, and I was now listening to her podcast with Michael Singer, author of *The Untethered Soul.* He was talking about the seer, the one who sees. As I walked looking onto the pathway stretching far ahead of me, I noticed there was a strangeness around me. It was as if I had walked through some invisible portal. I looked at my hands and was surprised at what I saw. It was as if someone else was looking at my hands through me. It was as if something very alien to me was looking through me. I could see every fine line on my hands and the tiniest hair follicles. Everything was so detailed. I slowed down, stopped, and slowly turned my hands around again and again. I stared at the brown colour of my skin. I had never seen it with such clarity and awareness before. It was so peculiar to look at my hands in this way that it scared me.

At that moment I remembered what I had read numerous times: I was not my body. My body was only a vessel—a physical form of me. I was observing it from a far vast place inside me like Deepak Chopra had talked about in the podcast the day before. Dr. Lees had also discussed becoming the observer in our sessions a decade ago, and I had read about it in Eckhart Tolle's book *The Power of Now*. Even though I had read and knew about the seer, I didn't experience it fully until now. I stared at my hands again oddly. I didn't know what to do next. My entire inside was so still. For a second, I thought, *Am I being taken over by something else? Am I losing my mind? What if it stays this way?* I put my hands by my side and slowly started walking. Wow, I had just met the seer inside me. I broke this state as I looked around at nature and walked back home.

Since that day, the one who sees comes and goes. I have a lot to discover from this spiritual journey I am on and many levels of my deeper self to uncover as I go. I have so much more to learn about my inner self and the divine forces at play within us all.

My Sweethearts, it was definitely the moment I broke my silence that unlocked the gate and allowed me to discover my inner self. Stepping into Dr. Lees' office immediately after helped me understand a little more. Then, I could see it, accept its existence, and take a step toward building a relationship with my true self and the Jeeti that I was. It carved a pathway for me to understand the horrific things that were done to my body were just that: things only done to my body, not the internal being that I am. My internal flame would always be lit; it could never be snuffed out by anyone or any horrific experience. It didn't matter what people thought, whether I was believed, or whether my parents and family stood by to support me. Connecting to my inner self helped me remember who I was and what my purpose was, and that was all that mattered. I moved forward with a definite knowingness that all would be well no matter what happened from that point forward. In fact, "All is well" became my mantra. The chorus of a Hindi song, "All Is Well," would play on repeat in my mind. I moved forward with a deep level of trust in myself and my abilities. I moved forward into the unknown that lay ahead with the knowingness that nothing could stop me. Of course there was fear, but I moved forward despite the fear. I let the knowingness guide me.

My soul is my inner compass that I must follow; I must obey its direction as it leads me to serve myself, my family, and humanity in a way that I didn't even know was possible. I have served my sisters and family well, and now it is my duty to serve my soul. To really tune into it, pay attention to it, hear what it's saying, see what makes it sing and dance, and understand its deepest desires. To let it follow its calling to be in service to other little girls, women, and the rest of humanity. The path of standing up for my truth, going inwards, claiming my power, and connecting with my spiritual self has helped me connect with a higher self that resides within. It has helped me understand and trust the messages coming from my higher self. It has helped me to check in with myself and ensure that I'm not some angry woman who is pissed off at the Kuta with a vendetta or ulterior motive. That isn't motivation enough for this work. I know I am not unjust in standing up for change in my brown culture and the world.

Embarking on a spiritual path is like having a wise teacher by my side. It has taught me so much about myself. Oh, my beautiful princesses, I can't tell you how imperative it is to connect with your inner self. To discover your inner beacon and to reap the benefits of aligning with your inner self. Without this connection you will remain lost and wander through life without any direction. Our inner guide lives within us as our greatest companion. To connect to it is vital because that is where true wisdom, strength, and unconditional love lies. The strength, guidance, and love we need to live through the most difficult challenges of life all can be found within our souls. Each of us is here to walk the Earth in our own brilliance, shine as a spark in the Universe, and learn lessons from experiences that come our way. Every experience will bring something new your way; the path of spirituality never ends.

Oh my darlings, explore this path with patience and an open heart. It's a wondrous, priceless journey into realizing your true power and potential—something you can harness to co-create with the Universe a life you love and deserve. I wish my Mom had passed on this wisdom to me. It truly is an awakening. As you grow you may think as I once did that the most important relationship is the one with your mother. My precious darlings, the most important relationship to have is the one with self. Everything else stems from there.

With Love,

Your Mommy

Jeeti

LETTER 25

Healing Is a Lifelong Journey

Dear Chandani,

My beautiful niece.

Or should I say Moonlight (the Punjabi meaning of your name). Your beautiful glow and beams of light have been a blessing in my life since I was 17 years old. I'm so glad Mom, who is your Nanni *(grandmother)* and my sister didn't give you away. They went against the advice of Dad, your Nanna *(grandfather)* to give you away to your father when your parents divorced—because you were a girl. I can't imagine how our lives would have been without each other.

You have seen and heard a lot in your lifetime. You have witnessed the pain and trauma your mom, your Kira Massi, and I have suffered. Of course, the effects of the trauma of sexual abuse trickled down to you, too. You saw your mom so angry and emotional while you were growing up, but you didn't know why. It all made sense to you once we broke our silence. From there, you witnessed the full load of blame, shame, and raw emotions that came with it. You watched family relationships tatter and wither away as if no love existed within them in the first place. You witnessed quarrels between me and my siblings and how the element of sexual abuse tore us apart. You saw what it was like for me, your mom, and Kira Massi to go through all the mudslinging and a very difficult, long court case. You saw how I had to weather it all, figure things out, and make decisions that would benefit my sisters too.

You saw it all up close.

I am so grateful to have a niece like you. You helped take care of your cousins, Shia and Maheema, who call you Didi *(sister)*, all the times I was off to court in Williams Lake. Of course you would, as I have been a huge part of your life ever since you were born. Oh, all the beautiful memories you and I have had together! Having sleepovers, spending weekends together, going out for breakfast, your Halloween costumes, and sharing fun summers together. Once when you were about 8 years old, I even took you to my class in university while I was babysitting you. You and I have shared so many precious moments in our lives. My heart beams watching you grow and go through the different phases of your life. You have been an integral part of my life. It's as if you are my third child. You have also witnessed me live through many phases of life, from being your Massi, to a wife, to a mother, to a business woman, to an advocate, to becoming a voice for others. You have watched me over the years go through my healing journey and the path to finding self, leaving behind footsteps that will inspire you, Maheema, and Shia to live life shining in your inner power.

I am so glad you were there to see it, Chandani.

It was a week after the verdict in April 2018 that my journey into self took a radical dive. A dear friend of mine named Sonja Picard had called to check in and see how I was doing after the long-awaited verdict. She said something I was not expecting.

"Take time off, Jeeti, to rest and heal," she encouraged me.

The court case saga had indeed been an exhausting, stressful, and emotionally draining rollercoaster ride. I was ready to sue the government, angry at a system that took so long to have the case heard and tried. I wouldn't rest until I took down the system that was at the mercy of the Kuta. It made me furious how long our case had taken in the Canadian justice system, a so-called developed country.

"Take 3 or 4 months off," my friend encouraged as I shared my thoughts. It was as if Sonja was holding a detour sign.

Three or four months? That's insane. What is she talking about? I thought. *Who takes that much time off for rest and recovery? Two or maybe three weeks,* I thought to myself, *was doable.*

She pointed me to the door of a local woman who used various modalities in her teachings. She thought it might aid me in my healing, rest and figuring out my next step, so I took the leap and committed myself to one of her workshops. Her name was Gila Golub, and I had no idea what I was getting into with her. Still, I trusted the Universe had sent her my way for a reason.

Boy was I right!

Working with the numerous modalities and tools she used in her work opened up massive golden gates into the self. Very quickly I realized just how right my friend Sonja was. I needed to rest. I needed time to heal and reset. It's interesting how the Universe sent Sonja at that exact moment to hold up the bright yellow detour sign right in my face, so I could take a much needed excursion into self and into awareness at another level. This was a journey that would take much longer than a few weeks. This was an unearthing, an excavation of old limiting beliefs and unconscious patterns, a letting go of and rewiring of new neural pathways and choosing differently. This journey would take a lifetime.

The concept of neuroplasticity (rewiring of the brain) and the door to self Dr. Lees had managed to crack open inside me set the stage for Gila's work to rip the vaulted door off its hinges. My comprehension of self, awareness and connection to Little Jeeti sored to a deeper level with her teachings. Finally, I was able to change the lens through which I saw myself. Now, I saw my innocence daily. And the more I saw my innocence, the more I could love and accept myself. I became more mindful of my thoughts and the voices in my head, and what they were communicating. I started to shift from a constricted belief system that knew only how to operate from intense fear to a belief system that came from a much more expanded place, a place of love. It blew my mind how drenched I was in fear and how deeply rooted it was within me at all times. My entire being had been running on an operating system fueled by fear.

It was shocking to realize, Chandani, how the old lens that I previously saw myself through was so limited, tainted, and distorted. I had unknowingly seen myself, the world around me, and others through the lens of poor me, a victim drenched in fear. How could I have known that? We are all programmed by our family, our culture, our institutions, and even society to operate from a place of fear. Add to that the fear and trauma passed down for thousands of years, generation after generation through our family of origin and epigenetics, and it's easy to understand why putting on a new lens may seem difficult. If fear is all we know, how can we see another way?

I saw more and more how I was conditioned and taught to please others, perform for them, compare myself, get an education, get married, have kids, be a perfect wife and parent, wear numerous hats, achieve so many things, and behave in a certain way as a female. I was told to always watch out for what people would think about me. I was taught that I would be valued by my social status, how big my house was, how fancy my car was, what I wore, how much money I had, and how obedient and perfect I was. I had lived with the knowingness of pleasing others, being a victim martyr, doing only what was best for the common good of the family, and being aware of the way others perceived me as a female. I had lived my entire life believing that love and validation came from the outside—the material things, the love and acceptance from others, the success in life. The concept of self-did not exist in this worldview.

By stepping into Gila's work, I connected all the pieces of what I had learned in Dr. Lees' office. All the books I had read now made so much more sense. Through Gila's work, I came to face my wounds head on—wounds I thought had ebbed and somewhat healed. I was shocked to see how huge and ripe they still were or that they existed inside me in this capacity still. I didn't know how badly these wounds were bleeding from all the endured trauma in my life and how they were preventing me from reaching my unlimited potential, unconditional love for self and the truth of who I was. Eventually, I came to see how they were affecting my every action. I had been looking for validation. I thought it was the job of my husband, my children, or others to make me feel special, worthy, whole, and complete. I had always thought I needed external love, strength, and support from my family members to survive. I came to learn, though, that what I craved and desired the most from others was something only I could give myself. It could only come from me. I could have it all, and I was worthy and deserving of having it all despite the story of my past. Whole hearted loving relationships, unconditional self love, unlimited abundance, and perfect health—I could have it all if I tapped into self love and total self acceptance.

I found that the more I saw my innocence, the easier it was for me to see the innocence of others. The more compassion I found for myself, the more compassion I was able to have for others. The more I accepted myself, the more accepting I became of others. I now had so much more compassion and empathy for my parents, my husband, my daughters, my siblings, and others. My perception started shifting. My brain was rewiring. My internal operating system shifted gears to be fueled by love instead of fear.

Now when I went on my walks, tears would flow down my cheeks. I could feel every cell in my body shed its own tears. These tears were different than the ones before. They were full of tremendous gratitude for all that I had in my life—the blessings, love, and abundance. My entire body would become flooded with joy, gratitude, love, and the richness of life and my inner power. I saw at a higher level the importance of daily gratitude and I became grateful for all the experiences life had brought me since birth. I learned how to connect deeper from a place of love for self and self acceptance. I started to see situations as an opportunity and became more aware of the expansive and unlimited space inside and around me. I felt my inner power surge through me as I expanded myself more and more. I could feel myself become more and more powerful within. My potential has become limitless.

Chandani, I couldn't believe how wrong I had it for all those years. I didn't need anyone else to accept, validate and praise me. It became crystal clear the only acceptance and validation I needed was from myself. The love and support I craved from my parents were the love and support I needed to give myself. The time to receive it from them was in my most formative years as a child, and that opportunity was long gone. No amount of love, support, validation, and attention from them now would fill the big, gaping hole that had formulated inside me since childhood. Only I could do that for myself. The ways I looked for my beloved husband Sohna to make me feel special, loved, nurtured and supported were the ways I needed to love, support, and make myself feel special. The love I craved to hear from him was the love I needed to say and give to myself. I had the power to give myself everything I needed. That was a very important and powerful realization for me—life changing in fact.

As I worked on my own self love and acceptance, I also began to see those that I felt had harmed me in a different light. I watched the anger, blame and judgments I had of them shift. I saw their own extensive wounding. The anger, hate, and toxic energy I felt toward them was being replaced with understanding and compassion. I could now look at my Grandpa's picture without flinching. I could look into my Mom's eyes without seeing them as his eyes. I also noticed the one who I had once called

Phaaji, Manjit, and the Kuta, I could now refer to as my cousin, Manjit Virk. I could refer to him with his given name without wincing at the sound of it. The anger, hurt, and painful emotions were shifting. I had opened the doorway into my heart to find compassion for all. Allowing it to bloom instead of keeping it constricted. I had stepped into the process of letting go.

My beloved niece, I have come to know that healing is a lifelong journey—an essential one if one wants peace. It is not an easy journey. It requires work and practice every day. Eventually, things do become easier. There is no instant fix, no magic pill that will instantly cure the trauma and take away the unease, and there is no fixed time limit. There are no shortage of triggers to take me back to the old familiar place of fear. My triggers will be my lifelong friends and my wounds will always be there, resurfacing from time to time. Now I have numerous tools from various modalities to deal with trauma and its symptoms, to help regulate my emotions and nervous system, dissipate and integrate trauma, and rewire my brain. One can never be completely healed, and my healing will continue until my last breath.

Finally, I see myself as worthy and deserving. I deserve to wear the crown—a crown I had hidden for so many years. I made myself small, afraid to stand in my true essence and inner power. Afraid of my own bright light. Now, that crown sits on my head in all its majestic glory. I wear it like a queen with pride, confidence, love, and grace. I walk forward on my path of creating a wonderful, prosperous life for myself despite my trauma and my story. I am listening to my soul, dancing with it passionately to life's wondrous tunes, doing the work that I love, and being the Great Mother I was meant to be.

I am excited you will continue to watch me grow and reach deeper layers of healing. As I move forward, I am thrilled you will continue to witness your Jeeti Massi chip away at and integrate deeper layers of pain and trauma. My library of inspiring and insightful books, podcasts, and workshops continues to grow, as do the self help tools in my toolbox. I'll be sure to share them all with you as you grow.

I am so glad you've been there to witness it all, Chandani.

With Love,

Your Massi

Jeeti

LETTER 26

You Can Choose

Dear M.V.,

You are my cousin.

You are my Dad's nephew.

You are the son of my Dad's second older sister.

You are Manjit Singh Virk.

You employed additional publication bans on the court case to prevent your name from becoming public. You hid behind the M.V. initials posted on the courtroom schedule. Frankly, you were trying to hide under the skirts of my sisters, cousin and me by using these bans in your favour.

You think you will fill the emptiness running through your being by using sexual abuse, assault, and rape as a medicine. You think you can cure your deepest wounds by harming those more vulnerable than you. You think lying, manipulating, and deceiving others is your greatest asset. You think that harming others and running away from taking responsibility is the only way.

It's never enough, is it? You can jump from person to person, as you did with me and my sisters, always looking to fill the wounds inside, but it's all a temporary fix. Your childhood wounds and the trauma you may have faced in your life remain. It's not pretty, is it? Whatever it is you feel deep inside is ugly. It's not easy for you to take responsibility, is it? It's easier for you to blame and shame others so you don't have to feel your own shame or blame. The biggest responsibility we have is to self, but you have no connection to self, do you?

Over the years, I watched you sit in your blindness in court. So many questions popped into my mind in those days.

What compels a human being to harm and violate another in abusive and sexually horrific ways?
What makes it right or okay in that person's mind?
How does that person justify his actions?
What is he searching for?
What is he trying to fill inside himself?

I may never know the answers, but I do know this: I have a choice. The choice is mine and only mine. I have the power to choose. I get to choose what kind of a mother I want to be to my girls. I get to choose how I want to show up for myself, for my family, or the world. I get to choose what qualities and values I hold, the kind of a person I want to be, and how I treat people. I get to choose if I want to come from a place of compassion and understanding for all those who commit harm on others and that includes you. I get to choose what work I put out there. I get to choose what thoughts or trauma play over again in my mind. I get to choose if I want to remain a victim to my past or do I simply let go and move forward in peace. I get to choose if I want to stay a victim as if the world is against me or if I want freedom. I get to choose something completely different—a life full of joy, peace, loving relationships, self acceptance, abundance, and good health where I wake up in my innocence every day.

I get to choose it all.

It truly is up to me to take the horrors of what has happened and use that knowledge to create a better life for myself, my girls, and my family. The traumatic experiences and the wounds the past have left behind are my greatest teachers. My wounds will be my life partners forever, rising from the shadows and making themselves welcome at any moment without warning. I get to choose to greet them from a place of love and compassion, to honour them, and to wrestle with them until I hear the message they are trying to convey. I get to choose to graciously see them out when the work is done and to let go of all that no longer serves me.

You have a choice too, Manjit.

You can choose to learn from your experiences.
You can choose to take accountability for your actions.
You can choose to stop harming others.
You can choose to heal your own wounds.
You can choose differently.

The question is, will you?

Truly,
Jeeti

LETTER 27

You Can Trust Women

Dear Madame Prosecutor,

A higher power must have been watching over me and my sisters to send you our way, Ms. Julie Dufour.

I first met you in February 2013 during our judicial preliminary inquiry in Williams Lake. Who knew back then how long we would travel together on this unbelievable roller coaster ride? Words cannot express my gratitude for all that you have done. I watched you work tirelessly, and I was in awe of how you were always so prepared to handle what went down in the courtroom. How you did your job and worked late hours while having a family of your own is beyond me. You were always over prepared and on top of everything, no matter what move, delay tactic, or loophole the defence used. You came in every morning well groomed and smiling with an alert mind and ready to go.

You stood by me and my sisters. You did your best to have our truths come out for justice and the safety of the public. You did not look at us Pooni sisters once with any ounce of doubt, judgment, blame, or shame. You believed me and did not treat me the way I had been treated by those who claimed they loved me. You looked me straight in the eye with kindness, care, compassion, and empathy. You were sincere and genuine with a curiosity to learn more about me, my family, and culture. You knew how to listen and hear every word I said. You had a passion and desire to do your job to the fullest, and you asked questions in a gentle, kind manner that would help you do your best. You came with a very compassionate and nurturing air, like that of a sister or a mother. You stood by me and my sisters in a manner no one else dared. Believing us, trusting us, understanding us, and acknowledging our pain was your goal. It was as if somehow you knew what it was like for us to have gone through rape, sexual abuse, and betrayal—as if you were somehow able to see and feel the pain and suffering. Of course, you would be able to do such a thing! You were a master of your work.

Your ability to create connection and rapport was splendid. You knew the power of creating relationships and trust in a case like this. Internally at first, I was standoffish with you. I was trying to read you and your niceness to make sure it did not come from a superficial place. In my mind, I questioned why you came and hung out with me and my sisters in the witness waiting room during the preliminary hearing. Why would you come to talk with us in those moments?

"In case I have to take over the case from the Crown prosecutor that is handling the preliminary hearing," you explained, as if you were reading my mind. "We like to be informed and know what is going on with each other's cases, so if for some reason the Crown on the case can't make it to court, then I would take her place."

From there the connection between us started to build. I eased my guard. Oh, how I loved seeing you before court and during the court breaks! You were so kind to give us updates anytime we asked. You have no idea what that meant to me. In an outdated, broken system, you showed me that someone really did care. To you, my truth mattered; I mattered.

It was this relationship of deep connection and trust with you that gave me courage and strength to continue with the court case when I grew tired of the courtroom drama as the years wore on. It's what helped me keep faith and continue forward no matter how difficult the journey ahead may be. You explained everything I needed to know and kept me up to date with what was going on in court. You answered my every question no matter how many times you had to explain it. You were very patient with me. You saw and understood the anguish my sisters and I were going through as we were dragged through the system for years. You treated me like a human being—like one of your own. I wasn't another case number or a file you had to clear off your desk. You genuinely cared about my case, your job as a prosecutor, and how me and my sisters had been horrifically violated. You were a white woman seeing me eye to eye, without any bias, judgment, or feelings about the brown colour of my skin. You treated me with dignity and respect. You admired my courage to speak my truth no matter what. You told me how smart I was. You proved to me there are good people in the system who want to see change and who can be trusted.

You are a rare gift to the world. All sexually abused people like me are blessed to have a person like you working for the good of humanity. You deserve more than a medal; you deserve the Order Of Canada. The criminal justice system needs more women like you. The world needs more women like you. We need more women believing and supporting women. We need women who actually care, want to make a difference, want to make the female voice be heard, and desire to see girls and women stand in their inner power. If only more women worldwide would stand up together as I felt you did for me and my sisters. What an impact it would have worldwide! Imagine what the world would look like for our girls if every sister, mother, grandmother, aunt, friend, and colleague stood up for each other. Imagine the courage, strength, and power it would generate down family lines if every mother, sister, and female stood up for girls.

Ms. Dufour, without question I can say I would not have made it through the trial without a passionate and deeply sincere Crown prosecutor like you. I don't think any other prosecutor could have done a better job! I would not be standing here today in the way that I am if it weren't for you. Without you my truth would have been buried in the loopholes and complexities of the criminal justice system, lost, muffled, and silenced once more.

I am extremely grateful to you!

Thank you from the bottom of my heart, on behalf of me, my sisters, my Pooni family, and my entire lineage for doing your best to help stop the cycle of abuse.

With Love,

Jeeti

LETTER 28

Awaken to The Great Ancestors

Dear Grandmothers, Great-Grandmothers, and Beloved Ancestors,

I close my eyes.

I see you. I feel you. I hear you.

I can see thousands and thousands of you in front of me, behind me, all around me. You are there all the way back into the horizon—that far off distance place where there is nothing but pure love and light—cheering me on, guiding, and supporting me with love. I feel you as a mighty force standing behind me—a force I can lean into for strength and courage and whose great wisdom I honour, especially when I am confused, scared, and overcome by fear.

My heart shatters when I think about the hard lives you all lived. I think about the trauma, fear, anger, frustration, and all the emotions you must have felt as you faced famines, wars, revolutions, droughts, and abuse of all kinds. I consider the unfortunate family situations and other unbearable living conditions caused by man or nature you had to endure. How must you have survived it all?

I didn't know breaking my silence and standing up for my truth would lead me to a place where I would be able to connect with you in ways I never knew. Through this connection I've been able to honour you with deep admiration and respect. Where there was once resentment, I now find gratitude and pride. I have such admiration for all you endured and the sacrifices you have made so I could have this life today. Connecting to you has helped me find more empathy and compassion for Mom and Dad and so many others who come from our culture.

The stones I saw being cast by others in my younger years had at some point been placed in my own hands. Without realizing it, I had picked them up from the ground myself and joined in throwing them as well. How did this happen? When did this happen? When I started believing the thoughts, beliefs, and judgments of others around me. When I started thinking of what others thought of me. When I started being "good" for Mom, Dad, the adults around me, and the outside world in order to get their love, attention, acceptance, and approval. When I started berating myself for being stupid, wrong, a complete disappointment, or impure. When I started believing the voices who told me that was true.

I was bewildered to see that in the crowded seats of the ancient coliseum where I had seen all the stone throwers, there sat the most familiar face on the majestic throne: my own. I too was sitting amongst the jeering crowd casting stones at the many versions of my younger self that stood in the arena below. I was shocked to see that it was I who was silently stoning myself. I was my own worst critic. I was throwing stone after stone by choosing to replay my past and the condescending voices in my head.

I am not good enough.
I am a disappointment, a disgrace.
I am unworthy, undeserving, imperfect, incapable, not smart, a complete failure.

The list went on. I was beating myself to death following the neural pathways of old limiting beliefs and feelings that brought me down to keep me in my place. They were feelings I had been carrying since birth. I was my own Grim Reaper.

Once I saw myself there and became aware of what I was doing, the stones automatically fell out of my hands. I was able to wake up and see it all clearly. My whole being filled with gratitude. I am so grateful to Mom and Dad for giving me the gift of life. I'm so glad they gave me this wonderful breath. Giving me breath was enough to get me into this world and to allow me to experience all that I have—the good, the bad, the ugly, and everything in between.

I am also grateful to my cousin Parm for the phone call and all her nasty words. Afterall, it was her phone call that shook me to my core and forced me to face my story and stand up for my truth. It was one of my biggest wake-up calls in my life—one of the greatest gifts sent to me by the Universe. It was because of her call that I broke my silence and connected to the Little Jeeti I was. Thanks to that call, I have been able to accomplish so much for myself, my daughters, my sisters, and my culture. I am grateful my wake-up call came in the form of unempathetic words from a woman I had loved instead of some deadly disease or something much worse. I have heard it over and over again from many great teachers: What you repress and refuse to express will find its way to express itself and manifest in your life in other ways. I am so grateful for all the experiences that have come my way to propel me forward to connect me with my soul and life's purpose. Thankfully, it is in this lifetime that I found the strength and saw the importance to stand up, heal the wounds that have been passed down from generation to generation, and stop the cycle of abuse in my family, my lineage, and my culture.

These words spell it out beautifully:

"Family dysfunction rolls down from generation to generation like a fire in the woods, taking down everything in its path until one person in one generation has the courage to turn and face the flames. That person brings peace to their ancestors and spares the children that follow."

-Terry Real

As you know, Great Ancestors, old ways, habits, perceptions, and ancient limiting beliefs that have been running through us for over thousands and thousands of years are hard to change. It's not easy. The unknown is scary for me. It would be easy for me to fall back into my comfort zone instead of moving toward the unfamiliar ahead. A part of me is afraid that I might lose all that I have—my marriage, family, life as I know it, and of course my identity as the familiar Jeeti I have been for all these years. It's so tempting at times to stay small and hidden from the world when these old feelings arise. However, I consider it an honour to become more and more aware of these feelings and the new identity I'm creating for myself. Many of them belonged to you and have been passed down to me through generations and generations. It's an honour to carry them with me wherever I go and to hold the space for these feelings when they arise. They are feelings that have been waiting to be felt and integrated for thousands of years. Feelings that are trying to tell me something about me and you. Feelings that are there to help me and future generations push through and grow to live our wildest dreams. Feelings that I get to integrate, transform, and let go of to allow myself to flourish and finally allow you to rest in peace.

I will honour you all and all the challenges you faced so I could have a better life. There is nothing more you want to see than me and my daughters living an abundant, healthy and prosperous life. I know you want to see the women in our culture thrive. I will honour you by doing just that. I promise to do my best to come from my heart, a place of love and compassion—the same love and compassion I see you glowing and bathed in way past the horizon into the ethers. And yes, I will be mindful of the intentions behind my actions.

I really do promise, Great-Grandmothers and Ancestors. I will move forward, embracing the divine energy, shining in my divine light, bidding the calling of my soul, and finally laying the stones to rest.

With Love,
Jeeti

The End

My story ends here for now.

As one chapter closes another begins. I will continue to share my journey as I co-create with the Universe to carve a new path.

Notes to the Reader

"scream
so that one day
a hundred years from now
another sister will not have to
dry her tears wondering
where in history
she lost her voice."

-jasmine kaur

LETTER 29

Be the Ripple

Dear Reader,

For those of you who have experienced the horror of rape and sexual abuse yourself, my heart feels your pain and trauma. I send you endless hugs full of love, inspiration, and light, enough for you to carry through this lifetime. I send you hope and prayers to find your innocence and inner peace. I send you courage to stand in your true self, confidence to move forward through life with your head held high, and strength to heal, grow, and live a prosperous and healthy life. By sharing my wounds with you and the details of my story, I hope to inspire you to find the path to your inner self, a path to healing, to blossom, and to live the life you were born to live. With every page you have turned and every letter you have read, I hope you've found solace knowing you are not alone. There are millions of us that share similar trauma. You, I, and the millions of others have endured suffering and pain together without knowing each other exists.

Yes, it is you that horrible things have been done to. It was you who was violated. Now, you are the one who has the power to heal yourself. You can choose to end your suffering and liberate yourself from the weight of the daily pain and trauma you carry. It is only you who can do the work to live a healthy life. It is not easy to bring into the light the pain and trauma trapped in your body. It does not dissipate or go away overnight. It may never even completely be resolved. It takes commitment and time to integrate. It is something you can chip at bit by bit, layer by layer. Healing is a journey—a journey that takes work, time, patience, love and compassion for self. It's a journey that will progress you through many phases: from anger to courage, victim to champion of one's own life, fear to love, pain to healing.

No matter which way your body and mind have been violated, you are precious. You matter. You are extraordinary. To live a whole and healthy life, it is vital to become aware of your wounds and heal. Only then can you help yourself, your daughters, your sisters, your mothers, your friends, and your communities. You need you, and the world needs you. You don't have to break your silence to the whole world. You don't have to march the streets in protest to rape and sexual abuse if you don't want to. You don't have to recount and relive every detail of your past. Having survived is enough. What's important is to accept and acknowledge your story to yourself, find your innocence again, and wholeheartedly accept and love yourself unconditionally just as you are. Being in this place emits new waves and ripples that will change the world inside and around you. You will radiate vibrations that will inspire you and those around you. From this place you will be a ripple that helps heal our planet.

For those of you whose bodies have never been violated, look around you. We who have been raped and sexually abused are everywhere. We live in your home, your family, your workplace, your local salon, your favourite coffee shop, your grocery store, your bank, your school. We are right there beside you when you walk down the street or drive on the highway. We are there at the park, concerts, skating rinks, and sporting events. We star in your favourite movies and music videos. We are your daughters, sisters, mothers, grandmothers, great-grandmothers, and ancestors. We are all genders. There is no escaping from us; we outnumber you by the millions.

Sadly, the ones who rape and commit sexual violence on others outnumber you, too. They are all around lurking everywhere you go. They live with you and amongst you as your sons, brothers, fathers, grandfathers, great-grandfathers, and your revered ancestors. They may even include the women in your life. You must open your eyes to them, too.

You may think the brutality of rape does not affect you, but it does indeed. The ripple effects of rape and sexual violence trickle into all of our lives. No one is spared from harm. For some the effects come in drops, but for others, it's like a tsunami sucking the life out of everything. The ripples of sexual abuse seep into every aspect of our society, culture, and country. No race, religion, or culture is spared from the effects. The perils and consequences of sexual abuse and rape and how it damages humans and society impacts you all, too. After all, as a collective, we are all one, so what happens to any one of us affects us all. Like a plague, it eats away at our communities and infiltrates our homes, families, schools, workplaces, institutions, and our minds. It infects our minds with demeaning beliefs and attitudes towards girls and women. Without you knowing, this mindset becomes deeply rooted in our society, infesting our laws, systems, and policies and tainting the lens of how we see others.

Whether you have been raped or not, we are in this together. We have created the kind of world we live in today, and we can definitely create a different one that ensures the safety, empowerment, and flourishing of everyone.

As a society overall, it seems we are vested in keeping the status quo. We're committed to laying blame and shame on the victim. What if I told you that culture and society have it all wrong? If one must blame someone, then we as humanity are all to blame. It is each and every one of us and the cultures we have created that owns this shame and blame.

One thing I know is that blaming, shaming, remaining silent, keeping quiet, or turning a blind eye is not the solution for eradicating the darkness that lurks in our homes and communities. These methods we have used for thousands of years haven't worked. They have failed us miserably. They have allowed the rape of women and children to become a pandemic. And now, it's time for us to wake up, open our eyes, and face this pandemic of rape, sexual abuse, and pedophilia straight on. It is time for us to hold ourselves accountable for what we allow in our homes and communities. It is time for us to heal our own minds, our own wounds, and our own families so we can build better communities, systems, institutions, and a loving world that serves us all.

Imagine what our families and the world would look like if we focused inward and looked at the pain, trauma, and darkness that resides in each one of us. If we all found our path to healing. The world would be full of love, understanding, compassion, peace, and oneness with all.

I believe we can get there.

We can continue the way we have for thousands and thousands of years. We can sit as bystanders in the ancient coliseum watching the silent stoning of little girls, boys, women, men, and people around us. Or, we can speak up, step out, and break the silence. We can stand up for the sake of ourselves and the ones around us who need it.

Which will you choose?

With Love,

Jeeti

LETTER 30

You Will Continue

Dear Reader,

Most of this book was written in 2017, much before the final verdict of the court case was released. Something compelled me to write the book before the verdict. I knew it needed to come from the voice that was speaking within me at the time. So much has transpired since the verdict in my own personal growth and healing. Coming out on the other side of it all has helped me shed a lot of layers. The lens through which I perceive my past, my wounds, myself, and others has changed. In many ways I feel different, evolved, enlightened, and more conscious. It's been an interesting exercise in letting go, embracing self, and sharing my experiences.

I have many reasons for writing this book, the first being to honour myself and the Little Jeeti I was. I wanted to acknowledge the suffering she endured and the suffering endured by my sisters, mother, aunts, grandmothers, great-grandmothers, and the great ancestors of my culture. I, of course, wanted to honour my daughters in this work. And yes, I wanted to answer the calling that is coming from my soul. To follow its yearning, be one with it, gracefully flow with its dance designed only for me, and carry out its bidding despite the consequences.

I have wrestled with what and how much to share with the world and if it's safe for myself, my daughters, and my sisters to do so. It hasn't been easy; my old self often struggles with my new self. I have had to face my darkest fears, but I knew I would never be at rest keeping all that I have witnessed and experienced to myself. Great insight and healing is passed down through breaking ancient codes of silence, shredding old sacred contracts that no longer serve us, bringing to light the dark hidden secrets through the power of storytelling, and thereby severing the old tethers that hold us back. It took tremendous courage and willingness to shred the old contracts I had with myself and others that no longer served me and my destiny. I wouldn't be able to live with myself if I locked my manuscript in a vault never to be found and shared.

I totally felt the sentiments of this poem from the book *Milk and Honey* by Rupi Kaur as I was reading it:

"our backs
tell stories
no books have
the spine to
carry"

The lived story, trauma, and suffering in my life and the lives of my sisters and family cannot be expressed in words and phrases encompassed in one book. There truly is no spine of any book that can carry the heaviness of the burden my sisters and I carried on our shoulders. There is no spine that can hold all the weight of the endured suffering encased in the words, paragraphs, pages, and chapters of my lived life.

Except that of my own spine.

I do hope in every word I have strung together that you hear, see, and feel the echoes of the voices of all those that have endured trauma and immense suffering.

I move forward in life in my true nature, illuminated in the rainbow of joy, love, grace, and peace. I continue dancing and co-creating with the Universe with a heart filled with curiosity and delight to witness the unfolding of the next chapters of my life. Indeed, life will be filled with ups and downs and challenges I have yet to face, learn, and grow from. Of course I would love for you to follow my journey as I venture out into the unknown, dancing in the steps and burning desire of my vibrant soul.

With Love,

Jeeti

P.S. The number one question I get asked is this: What can I do to support you? The one thing you can do is to sign up for 'A Note From Jeeti' to follow my journey and get information on upcoming projects. You can do that by visiting me online at jeetipooni.com. I would love your support in reviewing my book on Amazon and other retailers listed on my website to get the story of us #PooniSisters in the hands of those that will greatly benefit from it. I invite you to walk alongside us and witness my journey forward as we carry the torch of inspiration lighting up others across the world.

Follow me on:
Instagram: @jeetipooni
X (Twitter): @jeetipooni
Facebook: facebook.com/jeetipooni
Website: jeetipooni.com

Be sure to watch my documentary, *Because We Are Girls*, on Amazon Prime Video or Apple TV+ (available at time of publication in select countries), in Canada on the NFB Youtube Channel, or the NFB website at nfb.ca/film/because-we-are-girls/.

Acknowledgements

To Mom and Dad, for giving me life.

My sisters, daughters, and niece, the blessings in my life who love me exactly as I am and support my big, bold dreams.

My husband, for weathering the storms and challenges that have tested our love and commitment for each other.

Babbu Didi, for courage and support in standing alongside and breaking her silence.

My brother, who has done his best to be there for me.

My grandmothers, great-grandmothers, and ancestors, who endured so much so I could have this life today.

My grandfather, who watches over me every day.

My dearest friends and colleagues, who have loved and supported me.

My tribe worldwide, who sends me and us #PooniSisters messages filled with blessings, love, support, and courage to continue forward as hope and inspirational light.

My soul, who nudges me to move to its unparalleled dance steps.

And the Universe that guides me in every single moment.

Little Jeeti and all the different versions of me, who survived the many challenges.

About the Author

Jeeti Pooni broke her silence in 2006 when she realized her cousin, who had raped her and her sisters during their childhood, was potentially abusing others in her extended family. Jeeti and her sisters went on to endure one of the longest running sexual assault court case in Canadian history. The outcome found her cousin guilty but he eluded punishment.

Jeeti is a motivational speaker and the driving force behind The National Film Board of Canada documentary *Because We Are Girls*. Her mission as a social change maker is to advocate for criminal justice reform and overturn the passed down beliefs that shame and oppress women in her brown culture. She is a voice for those who suffer in silence and has inspired countless people worldwide to find their voice and speak their truth. Jeeti continues to motivate individuals to step up to become agents of cultural change to support survivors. She has been invited to speak across Canada and internationally about her experience.

Most importantly—and the primary reason for her journey for justice—Jeeti is a loving wife and mother of two daughters. Born in India and raised in Canada, she now lives with her family in British Columbia.

Manufactured by Amazon.ca
Bolton, ON

36252824R00152